D1379673

ROBERTS, SAMUEL KELTON, 1944-

SAMUEL K. ROBERTS

IN THE PATH OF VIRTUE

The African American Moral Tradition

THE PILGRIM PRESS
CLEVELAND, OHIO

E185.86
.R615
1999

To my sons,

Samuel Jr. and Franklin

The Pilgrim Press, Cleveland, Ohio 44115
© 1999 by Samuel K. Roberts

Published 1999. All rights reserved

Printed in the United States of America on acid-free paper

04   03   02   01   00   99   5   4   3   2   1

Library of Congress Cataloging-in-Publication Data

Roberts, Samuel Kelton, 1944–
    In the path of virtue : the African American moral tradition /
Samuel K. Roberts.
        p.   cm.
    Includes bibliographical references and index.
    ISBN 0-8298-1327-6 (alk. paper)
    1. Afro-Americans—Conduct of life.   2. Afro-Americans—Social
conditions—To 1964.   3. Virtue—History—18th century.
4. Virtue—History—19th century.   5. Social values—United States—
History—18th century.   6. Social values—United States—History—
19th century.   I. Title.
E185.86.R615   1999
179'.9'08996073—dc21
                                                        98-50615
                                                        CIP

CONTENTS

32378

AE N59 78

QUE 12 1500

NOV 1 4 2000

PREFACE

SINCE THEIR FORCED MIGRATION to the American shores, the Africans who eventually would become African Americans, and their descendants, have always had to contend with social forces that denied their right to live fully as human beings. Owned as chattel, exploited for their labor, they were viewed only as means for the economic betterment of their holders. And even for those who managed to secure freedom, popular ideologies and cultural myths were devised to justify their continued inferior class status. Indeed, during the period of slavery and for many decades thereafter, popular racial theories refused to ascribe to black people full inclusion in the human race, let alone full membership in the American body politic. Their humanity was essentially denied.

All African American social history is a chronicle of the struggle of a people to secure freedom and human dignity in a culture that was not always sympathetic to that aim. From outright slave insurrections to more subtle and personal forms of rebellion, on a corporate and individual level African Americans have sought to gain freedom and assert their humanity. Beginning with the Stono Rebellion in South Carolina in 1739, through the insurrections of Gabriel Prosser in 1800, Denmark Vesey in 1822, and Nat Turner in 1831, culminating with the wearing of Union blue by 180,000 free blacks and ex-slaves in the Civil War, a constant theme in the strivings of black people was the quest for freedom. Yet it must surely be affirmed that the quest for freedom must proceed from an altered social consciousness among the oppressed, a consciousness that denies the power of the oppressor to define another human being as a thing, a being less than human. Before any oppressed person can enjoy the freedom of the body, a revolution of sorts must be waged and won within the mind.

Some years ago, while researching the social thought of various African American thinkers and social activists in the first half of the nineteenth century, I was struck by the recurrence of the idea of virtue as they attacked slavery and injustice and sought to articulate the means whereby African Americans might gain a greater degree of social, political, and economic integrity. The reflections on virtue were not sterile ruminations on the nature of virtue as an abstract idea, but were affirmations about its role in life-and-death issues facing the African American community at the time, not the least of which was the fight against slavery. Speaking before a Boston audience in 1832, the abolitionist orator and activist Maria Stewart could declare that "never will the chains of slavery and ignorance burst, till we become as one, and cultivate amongst ourselves the pure principles of piety, morality and virtue."[1] Not quite twenty years later, the ex-slave and redoubtable stalwart in the struggle against slavery Henry Highland Garnet managed to combine a call to virtue with stiff resistance against oppression when he asked other blacks: "How shall we acquit ourselves on the field where the great battle is to be fought?" Answered Garnet: "By following after peace and temperance, industry and frugality, and love to God, and to all men, and by resisting tyranny in the name of Eternal Justice."[2]

One may sense within the appropriation of the concept of virtue, evidenced in the pronouncements of just these two thinkers—Stewart and Garnet—the full range of social and ethical mandates that would be voiced as African Americans in the eighteenth and nineteenth centuries reflected on the meaning of virtue in their personal lives and its portent for the destiny of the race: personal rectitude coupled with zeal to combat slavery and oppression; moral purity with economic and political uplift. Moreover, as this book will affirm, historic reflections on the role of virtue in African American life provided the means to ensure a level of public discourse within the African American community so that urgent matters such as political and economic uplift—and indeed race survival—might be discussed, debated, and put into sharp focus. Reflections on virtue were also celebrations of the humanity of black people at a time when the American legal system and the more informal structures of American culture denied the full worth of that humanity. Thus, there emerged an integral relationship between a meditation on virtue—and the virtues—and the socially urgent demand to devise ways to ensure a socially viable life.

This book, therefore, is an attempt to explore how black people came to understand and appropriate this classical idea of virtue as they sought to counter the regnant cultural and legal institutions that denied and brutalized their humanity. Indeed, inasmuch as virtue could inspire resistance to oppression and provide a rich foundation for community building and the nurturing of the personal and communal spirits of black people, the social consciousness of African Americans, so necessary for their survival and, ultimately, their transformation from bondage to freedom, was greatly enhanced.[3] Of such is the consuming passion of this work.

Many persons have sustained and encouraged me over the years as this project has taken shape. I must thank the staff of the Schomburg Center for Research in Afro-American Culture of the New York Public Library and the Moorland Spingarn Collection at Howard University for valuable assistance during the early years of research related to this project and that of the William Morton Smith Library in Richmond. My colleagues at Union Theological Seminary more than twenty years ago, Professors Cornel West, James Cone, James Forbes, and the late James Washington, offered valuable responses during the formative stages of the thesis. Geraldine Fisher and Valerie Hermoine Fisher showed immense patience during many years of discussing the idea, as did my sons, Samuel Jr. and Franklin, to whom this book is dedicated. Countless persons who have been forbearing enough to hear me out even when the ideas were still inchoate must be thanked as well. I must thank my colleagues on the faculty of the School of Theology of Virginia Union University for their comradeship and support, and especially Dean John W. Kinney for finding the resources to support a sabbatical leave during which time I was able to complete the manuscript. I must thank as well Timothy Staveteig and Ed Huddleston of The Pilgrim Press for their unflagging encouragement and keen editorial discernment. Finally, my partner now in life and vocation, Judith Mayes Roberts, has been an undying source of care, nurture, and delightful dialogue. For these gifts of her person, I shall forever be grateful.

Attend me, Virtue, thro my youthful years!

O leave me not to the false joys of time!

But guide my steps to endless life and bliss.

—Phillis Wheatley,

"On Virtue" (c. 1770)

1

VIRTUE AND
AFRICAN AMERICAN
EXISTENCE

"Lord, I want to be a Christian, in my heart, in my heart."

American Negro spiritual

WHEN CONFRONTED with apparent contradictions, moral enigmas, or absurdities, human beings always tend to respond by seeking or creating meaning systems that can explain, mitigate, or put in satisfying perspective the enigmas at hand. We are above else creatures who need to have the world explained *to* ourselves *by* ourselves. We need to set before our eyes the explanations and resolutions of deep enigmas. Whether through religious systems, philosophical musings, or artistic creations, we must seek explanations and resolutions of the great moral and spiritual problems of life.

Within the part of the African American experience that was grounded in slavery, enigmas, contradictions, and perplexing absurdities have abounded. Captured Africans surely must have asked what quirk of destiny had consigned them to a brutalized form of existence thousands of miles from their native countries and cultures. Generations upon generations of black slaves in this country must have pondered whether some divine explanation lay behind the failure of liberation to come. Many were surely like Louis Hughes, born into slavery in 1832 in Virginia. After four attempts to flee

1

from slavery, Hughes finally succeeded during the closing months of the Civil War, escaping to refuge behind Union lines not far from his holder's estate near Memphis. In his memoirs, written as an older man in 1897, Hughes could still recall how "it [this freedom] had been talked about from generation to generation."[1]

Slaves were forever conscious of the inherent contradictions of slavery and the racism that supported the institution. An essay on slavery written by an anonymous black man who gained his freedom sometime after the turn of the nineteenth century quite eloquently attacked this aspect of the institution with bitter irony: "I am one of that unfortunate race of men who are distinguished from the rest of the human species by a black skin and wooly hair—disadvantages of very little moment in themselves, but which prove to us a source of greatest misery, because there are men who will not be persuaded that it is possible for a human soul to be lodged within a sable body."[2]

The same "free Negro" went on to lodge another charge against the institution of slavery. After painstakingly refuting the notion of the innate inferiority of blacks (along the way marshaling the pathos of Shylock's soliloquy: "Has not a Negro eyes? Has not a Negro hands, organs, dimensions, senses, affections, passions?"), the author indicted slavery for its tendency to undermine the moral integrity of the one enslaved: "Cruel that you are! You make us slaves; you implant in our minds all the vices which are in some degree inseparable from that condition; and you then impiously impute to nature, and to God, the origin of those vices, to which you alone have given birth, and punish in us the crimes of which you are yourselves the authors."[3]

Having thus indicted slavery for its tendency to warp the moral integrity of the enslaved, the former slave avowed that "the condition of the slave is nothing more deplorable than in its being so unfavorable to the practice of every virtue." What a startling denunciation of slavery! It affirms that slavery is more than a political or civil matter in which one person presumes to rob another of his or her labor and substance; slavery is a moral affront in that it frustrates and undermines the ability of the enslaved to practice and embody virtues, virtues that presumably when practiced would be within the provenance of self-possessing, viable human beings. Thus, the appeal to the practice of virtue becomes in the mind of this anonymous black writer a powerful rebuke to the institution of slavery.

Virtue is a long-standing idea in moral theory. It was foundational to classical Greek moral philosophy, particularly as postulated in the Platonic and Aristotelian traditions. Platonic thought held that four primary virtues—reason or prudence, justice, fortitude, and temperance—enabled the soul, as an organism, to moderate and govern successfully the often warring impulses or appetites plaguing it. Aristotelian thought, taking a much more inductive tack through actual observation of human beings, held that virtue helped us fulfill our function as living beings. What is our purpose or function as living beings? It is to live well. And to be sure, for Aristotle, living well belongs to the realm of human activity that is vigorous, well proportioned, discerning, and courageous. Persons of virtue are motivated by a unitary vision for living (temperance), able to use powers of discernment (prudence) to act reliably and consistently (fortitude) in courses of action consistent with equity (justice).

Christian tradition, primarily as a result of the Augustinian embrace of Platonism and Thomas Aquinas's appropriation of Aristotelian concepts, would affirm the classical virtues as fundamentally consistent with Christian moral sensibilities, terming them "cardinal" virtues. These virtues were deemed cardinal because they formed the hinge (*cardos*) on which the possibilities of leading a full, vibrant, and meaningful (Christian) life depended. Indeed, as Josef Pieper, a contemporary thinker in the field of virtue ethics has put it, the cardinal virtues enable us to "attain the furthest potentialities of [our] nature."[4]

African Americans who were engaged in the struggle against slavery and in the struggle to affirm racial uplift in the years after slavery held to a concept of virtue that may be defined in this way: virtue became a vision of a divinely ordered life that impelled its adherents to struggle against the injustice of slavery and to forge communities and structures that could ensure the development of the furthest moral and material possibilities of African Americans. Adherents to this notion of virtue were able to use powers of discernment to determine right actions and fashion a vision of life as a powerful rebuke to the system that sought to deny them full humanity. They believed that as human beings, they ought to be free. Slavery offered a life devoid of any good end from the perspective of the enslaved; it was a life devoid of self-possession. Virtue, on the other hand, held out the promise of a life of self-possession, a life lived in pursuit of actions consistent with a free person's conceived good end or purpose in life.

For early African American thinkers who sought to affirm their being when institutions and persons surrounding them constantly denied such being, the attraction to the idea of virtue seems reasonable. One of the purposes, therefore, of this chapter is to discern historical patterns and contemporary expressions of the search for virtue within African American social consciousness, a conception of virtue that has provided a measure of wholeness in life, an organizing principle of life, a counterweight to racist dogma that denied that black people had any right to "the good life." The historical experiences of those Africans and their descendants, slave and free, whose lives and fortunes became intricately enmeshed in the total American experiment, form the backdrop against which the search for African American patterns of virtue proceeds.

Slavery, Racism, and the Assault on Black Being

Racist society has sought to impose a state of nonbeing on black Americans. In its efforts to do this, the racist society exemplified in the slave system and in the subsequent caste system that replaced slavery after emancipation has sought to impose two conditions upon blacks: a state of contingency and a state of precariousness. "Contingency" is here understood as a condition of utter dependence upon another, rendering a person devoid of any basis for self-governance or a sense of autonomy. A state of "precariousness" is imposed upon someone so that person is forced to live in a fundamentally unstable condition or a condition in which a person has no power to impose a sense of order on her existence.

Such were the desires of racist society as it sought to make the alien African a slave, to maintain slavery and to maintain power arrangements that resembled the status quo ante even after the end of slavery. The quest for virtue functioned for the African American as an organizing principle around which to mount actions to counter contingency and precariousness. Moreover, the quest for virtue was an attempt to inject a measure of wholeness in African American life, a measure of moral vitality and integrity.

The initial contacts between the earliest white settlers in North America and the Africans who involuntarily joined them there were marked by mutual suspicion, fear, and a profound wonder about how the world into which each was thrust would eventually take shape. The call of a Dutch man-of-war ship at the English colony of Jamestown in 1619 and its discharge of nineteen "negars" began the torturous path of relationships between whites and blacks in this country.

In early colonial society, the social and racial hierarchies had not yet solidified as they would toward the end of the seventeenth century. Before that time, it was not clear whether Africans were considered slaves or indentured servants, as so many English people were. There is evidence that blacks could escape the lowest ranks of society, become free, and own property. Anthony Johnson, who had been shipped to Virginia in 1621 and worked as a slave on a James River tobacco plantation, survived a 1622 assault by Native Americans on the colony, eventually gained his freedom, and became a large landholder, moving to the colony of Maryland by the 1660s. More than a few blacks of that era "lived as assertive men and women who acquired property, formed families, and provided for their children's welfare."[5]

By the 1660s, however, the same time when Anthony Johnson could begin his homestead in Maryland with some degree of confidence about the future, developments were occurring that would dash any hopes of blacks to secure a place as full members of colonial society. The need for cheap labor on the burgeoning plantations, in addition to the dwindling supply of white indentured servants and the increasing and ready availability of captured Africans from the West Indies, produced the conditions in which blacks could no longer hope to escape servitude. Social and legal barriers were soon erected to prevent the possibility of blacks' mobility from servitude to freedom. By 1691, freed black slaves were banished from Virginia altogether.

Even in the North the slavery of blacks assumed an increasing level of social regularity. Although the Massachusetts Bay Colony prohibited slavery and considered itself a haven for persons fleeing famine, war, and persecution, a 1641 statute did not protect from bondage persons who were "lawful captives taken in just wars, and such strangers as willingly sell themselves or are *sold to us*."[6]

Alien Africans became the exclusive group of persons falling into the last category, that of "strangers . . . sold to us," those consigned to perpetual bondage. Consequently, slavery became the general and prevailing norm of the vast majority of blacks born in this country and those forcibly brought here. By the time of the American Revolution, all thirteen colonies had some slavery laws; however, the practice played a lesser role in the North than it did in the South.

Thus, the fate of either being considered outright chattel or being consigned to a pariah class of nominally free persons was the lot of the descendants of the first Africans who came upon the American shore in 1619. The primary thesis of this chapter and indeed the central argument of this book is that because of the inherent nature of slavery and the contempt with which the dominant racial community has historically regarded the free black community, the racist impulse of America has perpetually attempted to impose a state of contingency upon blacks.

The attempt to impose contingency, *if successful,* would strip African American consciousness of its inner source of generativity and life. However, the purposeful rejection of this attempt grew, as we shall see, out of an attempt among black Americans to construct an organized way of life, a vision of the good that would go beyond the mean-spirited attitudes of oppressive whites. African Americans endeavored to seek the virtuous life and, in so doing, affirm their being in the face of efforts to deny that being.

The Attempt to Impose Contingency and Its Rejection

The dynamics of contingency directed against blacks were perhaps first manifested in the calculated effort to strip slaves of their will. One of the basic assumptions of the slave system was that the slave, viewed as chattel property, existed to provide labor for others who owned the slave or had direct claim to such labor. The slave was theoretically an appendage of the owner; a slave was a mere extension of the will of the holder.

The hoped-for destruction of the slave's will and its complete mastery by the master constituted the main reason for the infamous "seasoning" process that awaited the African captives at the end of the Middle Passage, that harrowing voyage across the Atlantic on slave ships. In preparation for a life of slavery either in North America or in the Caribbean, the slaves were put through an incredible regimen of brutalizing labor, gratuitous punishment, and physical torment calculated to break the spirit and instill a sense of terror and fear of the whites. Such seasoning, to the extent that it worked, produced not so much docile slaves as demoralized slaves.

The violence done to the slave's will was the first stage in the attempt to impose contingency. The slave whose will was constantly attacked and brutalized was thus deprived of the means by which he was able to determine his future and the shape of his present. The ability to do that was relinquished or was seized by an oppressive other—a master or an overseer. The other, who by virtue of the ideology of the slave system, had no reason to respect the existential integrity of the slave or to allow that the slave had an independent mind and will. Had masters or overseers acknowledged or encouraged self-willful acts on the part of slaves, they would have eradicated the crucial difference between free men and slaves: *the freedom to act according to one's will.*

Henry Bibb, in reflecting on his life of bondage, painfully understood this link between the desired subjugation of his will by his holder and his subsequent inability to exercise control over his personal existence:

> As a slave, I was subjected to the will and power of my keeper, in all respects whatsoever. That the slave is a human being, no one can deny. It is his to be exposed in common with other men, to the calamities of sickness, death and the misfortunes incident to life. But *unlike* other men, he is denied the consolation of struggling against external difficulties such as destroy the life, liberty, and happiness of himself and family.[7]

Austin Steward recalled bitterly his sense of contingency when he pondered the slave's "uncertainty of his future, over which he has no control."[8] For the slave, therefore, all of time—the present and the future—belongs theoretically to the slave owner and is controlled by his or her will. Holding power over the slave's time was a manifestation of contingency. Perhaps for this reason the ability of slaves to "hire out" their own time took on such universally important social significance. Being able to hire out their time represented a small victory in slaves' relentless struggle to seize what degree of personhood the slave system could afford.

To be sure, in slavery as in most social institutions there was some degree of flexibility and elasticity. Pressure to effect such flexibility came from the slaves themselves, who used every means at their disposal to exercise resistance to the system. Slave owners and overseers were constantly plagued by such resistance: malingering, creation of diversions, sabotage of work tools, self-mutilation. In such ways slaves sought to counter the oppressive power of their masters and the contingency they sought to impose upon them.

But despite the countless ways devised to "beat the system," the brutal reality of slavery was ever present in the consciousness and in the everyday life of the slave. Restriction of free movement was commonplace; punishment remained very much a certainty if caught breaking the rules, however trivial the infraction; separation from dear ones was always a possibility; being sold was not to be ruled out. Bondage was a fact, unless escape or death ended the misery. And as long as the structures of bondage were firm and in place, the process of imposing contingency took its course.

Within typical human relations there is a state of mutual dependence and reciprocity in interaction. Reciprocity means that a state of mutual obligation exists between persons; a give-and-take interaction is implied. Inherent in this situation is the self-awareness that one is called upon to consider the rights and feelings of others *before* taking significant action. All human beings seek a level of reciprocity in interaction with other people. The assumption of these intricate, often unstated "contracts" of reciprocity becomes the very foundation of the social bond.

A state of reciprocity is no longer assumed in a situation in which one person desires to impose contingency on another. In the actual world of slaves and masters, contingency is experienced when the slave becomes a victim of capricious acts of the master. Even when a slave fulfills his assigned role of keeping his "place" as a slave, he is not assured of the master's positive response. While bondage itself is vile, the violation of the delicate network of hoped-for mutuality seems to the slave to be an additional outrage. There is a sense of betrayal, of going beyond the limits of human decency. And the slave senses this as an essentially wrong state of affairs.

Austin Steward, for much of his early life a slave, reflected that slavery's "bitterness arises from a consciousness of wrong; a sense of violation of every right God has given to man."⁹ Such a wrong could be done because of the master's possession of a disproportionate amount of power over the slave. This legal and actual power of the master over the slave would diminish or frustrate any natural tendency toward mutuality of dependency between the two. And tragically, the areas of life that were most dear to the slave—the sense of self, bonds between mate and children—could fall victim to the power of the master when his power led him to attempt to impose contingency upon the slave.

Frederick Douglass understood the underlying aim of American slavery as stripping slaves of their wills and depriving them of any sense of mutuality with others who have power over them. After securing his own freedom, Douglass could share his bitter reminiscence of slavery with an audience in 1850 in this way: "The first work of slavery is to mar and deface those characteristics of its victims which distinguish men from things, and persons from property. It reduces man to a mere machine. It cuts him off from his Maker, it hides from him the laws of God, and leaves him to grope his way from time to eternity in the dark, under the arbitrary and despotic control of a frail, deprived, and sinful fellow-man."¹⁰

Douglass went on to affirm that the slaveholder must destroy an internal propelling power before complete control over the slave is accomplished. "As the serpent-charmer of India is compelled to extract the deadly teeth of his venomous prey before he is able to handle him with impunity," explained Douglass, "so the slaveholder must strike down the conscience of the slave before he can obtain the entire mastery over his victim." Contingent persons can never become whole, viable persons as long as the power to effect their will remains in the possession of another, whose power knows little of limiting bounds.

Related to contingency is another characteristic endemic to slave existence—precariousness. Precariousness connotes the presence of danger as a result of a fundamental state of instability. A circus audience perceives precariousness in the tightrope walker's act because of the illusion of instability, especially if there is no net underneath. Instability, however, was no illusion in the life of the slave. There was perhaps no greater symbol of precariousness than the ubiquitous auction block. It was the terrible vehicle for sending loved ones away, or being sent away, from familiar surroundings to strange new places.

Such was the case especially among the states of the upper South, where toward the middle of the nineteenth century the need for large numbers of slaves on plantations lessened, thus encouraging some planters to breed and export slaves to the Deep South. Doubtless, a sense of dread must have filled the hearts of people who had attempted in many ways to follow a basic human tendency—to establish stability in patterns of family and friendship .

In reminiscing on his years as a slave before his escape, J. W. C. Pennington concluded that "one of the chief annoyances of slavery, even in the most mild form, is the liability of being at any moment sold into the worst form."[11] Austin Steward, whose master was forced to sell off assets of his estate because of horse-racing debts, felt similarly:

> We had heart-felt emotions to suppress, when we thought of leaving all that was so familiar to us, and chose rather to "bear the ills we had, than to fly to those we knew not of." And oh, the terrible uncertainty of the future, that ever rests on the slave, even the most favored, was felt with a crushing weight. Today, they are in the old familiar cabin surrounded by their family, relatives and friends; tomorrow, they may be scattered, parted forever. The master's circumstances, not their own may have assigned one to the dreaded slave-pen, another to a distant race swamp; and it is this continued dread of some perilous future that holds in check every joyous emotion, every lofty aspiration, of the most favored slave at the South.[12]

No human bond—the marriage tie, the sibling bond, the friendship pact—was completely exempt from being severed by the auction block. All of the relations that in normal societies enjoy some degree of stability could be shattered with the thud of an auctioneer's gavel. For whatever reason, for punishment or for payment of debts of a financially incompetent master, being "bid in" on the auction block was a distinct possibility for many slaves.

Enslaved blacks have, with varying levels of success, always devised means and ways to establish socially stable bonds among themselves. Herbert Gutman's now classic study of the African American family during slavery and the vast array of strategies used to preserve marital and familial bonds documents this will to counter attempts to impose social precariousness. But perhaps even at the most elemental level of social organization, the dyad—two persons maintaining a significant relationship—exhibited the will to construct and maintain social order and the basis for community.

Anthropologists Sidney Mintz and Richard Price, engaged in what might be termed historical anthropology, have investigated the cultural patterns of blacks in the Caribbean and have discovered that friendship pacts formed in the holds of slave ships often lasted for life, or as long as physical proximity would allow. Such friendships, formed when both persons were forcibly separated from family and village, often took on a close bonding like blood kinship. The use of familial terms, "sis" and "bro," were common. The kinship was possible because the Africans brought with them a concept of kinship that allowed even cousins twice removed to consider themselves brothers or sisters.[13] When faced with the absence of real kinspersons, they modeled the new social ties upon those of kinship.

Many slaves attempted to forge a degree of marital and familial stability, yet the very nature of the slave system meant that such attempts constituted an uphill struggle. The system dictated that the extension of the master's will, rather than that of the slave father, husband, mother, or wife, had to assume priority. To the extent that the practice of virtue was inherent in developing familial bonds, slavery acted as a corrosive element. An anonymous "free Negro," the author of the essay "Slavery," wrote, "The surest foundation of virtue is love of our fellow-creatures; and that affection takes its birth in the social relations of men one to another. But to the slave these are all denied. He never pays or receives or experiences the fond solicitude of a father—the tender names of husband, of brother, and of friend, are to him unknown."[14]

In the area of basic relations forged in familiar physical surroundings, precariousness was an inherent aspect of the slave system. But more than this aspect of precariousness, there was a psychological side that could be equally debilitating. The master class consciously instilled this kind of precariousness in the slave population to ensure that as much as possible slaves deferred to masters and the ideology of the slave regime for their notions of legitimate order (i.e., notions of what was right and moral, which in a weirdly ironic way justified their own contingent positions). In some cases it worked, especially among slaves whose sense of pride and worth was measured in relation to the social proximity to their masters.

In Frederick Douglass's autobiography, he remembered how some slaves of planters of high economic status would assume an air of superiority over the slaves of masters of lesser social rank. Such slaves reflected the values of the oppressor class and found a curious sense of social stability in doing so. Slaves who betrayed other slaves seeking to escape or organize an uprising obviously reflected the values of the master class. Their behavior was an indication that the perimeters of life were determined by an *oppressive other* who sought to render another human being an enslaved, contingent person. Such a condition, such behavior, grew in the soil of self-hatred.

"The slave looks around in vain," mused the anonymous free Negro, "to find a being more wretched than himself. He can indulge no generous sentiment—for he sees himself every hour treated with contempt and ridiculed, and distinguished from irrational brutes by nothing but the severity of punishment." It would not be surprising, then, continued this writer, "if a slave, laboring under all their disadvantages—oppressed, insulted, scorned, trampled on—should come at last to despise himself—to believe that it would be against his nature to cherish any honorable sentiment or to attempt any virtuous action."[15]

The slave system was designed to impose a functional state of contingency upon black people. Although that system could never impose ultimate contingency on all of its victims to the same degree or render all slaves completely contingent, the physical restraints of free exercise of limbs and will meant that unless mitigated by counter forces, a state of some degree of contingency prevailed in the slave experience.

The efforts to produce an integral ethos in the slave community independent of the white, slave-owning community were efforts, seen in the context of our thesis, to counter attempts to impose contingency. If the slave community could devise and nurture and sustain a set of values, myths that derived from its own spiritual energy and not that of the whites, then in some measure contingency would be lessened. The imposition of contingency will succeed best within persons bereft of cultural and spiritual moorings.

Sterling Stuckey reports from his studies of black folklore that slaves still were able to maintain a store of values and a lifestyle that had vitality and integrity apart from the world of the masters. In his words, "slaves were able to fashion a life-style and a set of values— an ethos—which prevented them from being imprisoned altogether by the definitions which the larger society sought to impose."[16] The peculiar vision of virtue in the minds of African American adherents is part and parcel of such values.

But what of the nominally free black community, especially the free black community in the northern states? Was it subject to the attempts to impose contingency as well? A small proportion of free blacks always existed at any given time in the history of America. Their freedom had been acquired by escapes to freedom, by manumission by owners, or by acts of heroism performed during extraordinary circumstances, as in a state of war, most notably in the War of Independence or in the War of 1812. Such free blacks numbered 59,000 at the time of the first decennial census taken in 1790 and increased steadily thereafter. By 1830, at a time when the articulating of virtue as a means of combating slavery and advocating racial uplift would be in full bloom, fully 122,000 free blacks were in the nation, mainly in the northern states.

But the free blacks led a rather tenuous existence at best and were considered outcasts in many places at worst. In the first place, the North was not uniformly hospitable to blacks. As late as 1800 there were 36,000 black slaves in the North, most of them in New York and New Jersey.[17] When abolition did finally come to all of the northern states, a lingering residue of legal and semilegal restrictions and popular animosity against blacks made life quite severe for the free black community. Politically, they were not full citizens in that the right to vote was not always granted. The extension of property rights, protection in the courts, and other civic privileges could not always be presumed.

Martin Delaney, who after 1851 so despaired of any hope of the free black community being treated with equity in the United States that he became a strong advocate of emigrationism, pondered whether there were any political differences between the nominally free black community and that of the enslaved community, and he concluded that there was very little difference:

The bondman is disfranchised, and for the most part so are we. He is denied all civil, religious, and social privileges, except as he gets by mere sufferance, and so are we. They have no part nor lot in the government of the country, neither have we. They are ruled and governed without representation, existing as mere excrescences on the body politic—a mere dreg in the community, and so are we. Where then is our political superiority to the enslaved?[18]

Moreover, in many respects the life chances of free blacks in the North and South were just as miserable and circumscribed as those of slaves. While free blacks in the North and South were not legally enslaved, the social and economic constrictions placed upon them produced a condition similar to chattel slavery. Economically, free blacks were often the victims of the prejudices of not only native whites but also immigrants, both of whom saw blacks as despised competitors for jobs. Those who escaped slavery and probably had acquired some skills often found difficulty using such skills in an economy infused with white prejudice. While there were small merchants and shopkeepers among the free blacks and thus some degree of economic viability, discrimination in hiring practices relegated the vast majority of black workers to menial positions—day and common laborers, porters, servants, washerwomen, and stevedores. All of these factors meant that for the most part the free black community was an economically marginal community.

They could not be bought or sold away from families, but they were often the victims of forced expulsion as in the case of the aftermath of the Cincinnati race riot of 1829. And tales of kidnapping northern blacks for the southern slave markets permeated most free black communities in the North, even into the 1850s, especially after the passage of the Fugitive Slave Act of 1850. "In the Northern states we are not slaves to individuals, not personal slaves, yet in many respects," thought members of the Colored National Convention of 1848, "we are the slaves of the community." These words expressed the grim realities for free blacks and the degree of opprobrium with which their countrymen and countrywomen held them. The existential mood of free blacks in the context of white hostility and indifference was stated with poignant eloquence by the following: "We reside among you and yet are strangers; natives, and not citizens; surrounded by the freest people and most republican institutions in the world, yet enjoying none of the immunities of freedom. . . . Tho we are not slaves, we are not free."[19]

The slave and the free black communities found themselves, therefore, in varying degrees adversely affected by the attempts of racist society to impose contingency and precariousness upon them. Those conditions, as perceived by slaves and nominally free blacks, created situations that were obviously antithetical to the development of whole, viable human beings. The specter of contingency violated the quest for human wholeness.

Virtue, Viability, and the Free Life

If contingency is the most prominent trait of the enslaved life, then viability may be conceived as the essence of the truly freed life. "Viability" suggests the capability of sustaining independent life. Viability may be understood as the quality of existence without which a person or group is devoid of an interior generative force capable of achieving and sustaining life. Without viability a person may be seen as being driven and sustained from without.

This notion of viability suggests the view of virtue as expressed earlier in this chapter. Among African Americans who were engaged against the evil of slavery and the attempts by racist society to render them contingent, virtue was understood as a divinely ordered life that impelled its adherents to struggle against injustice and oppression and to forge communities and structures that could ensure the development of the furthest moral and material possibilities of African Americans. That virtue was lived out within the crucible of the often hostile America as they knew it.

We have already noted that the classical understanding of virtue was a vision of the excellence of human character as evidenced in four dimensions: prudence, temperance, fortitude, and justice. The African American articulation of virtue implicitly affirmed this tradition but, within the crucible of slavery and oppression, was able to transform a classical idea into a vision for living that defied attempts to deny the humanity of black people.

Let me hasten now to sketch the outlines of this notion of virtue before it is given a fuller historical development in the following chapters.

In the first half of the nineteenth century, African American public speakers such as Maria Stewart, William Hamilton, the members of the American Moral Reform Society, and firebrand essayists such as David Walker celebrated the power of the *disciplined intellect* as a weapon in the arsenal to be used against slavery and oppression. In 1833, Maria Stewart, perhaps the first American woman to assume the public podium in the fight against slavery, told an audience in Boston that she felt compelled to speak out because blacks were "looked upon as objects of pity and commiseration." Accordingly, her soul had been filled with a "holy indignation" forcing her to come forward "and endeavor to turn their attention to knowledge and improvement, for knowledge is power!"[20] Rev. Amos Gerry Beman must have stirred an audience more than a quarter of a century later when he advised, "To be ignorant is to be weak, and to be weak is to be miserable."[21] A disciplined intellect would surely sharpen powers of discernment, powers enabling the black community to negotiate the treacherous and torturous pathway that lay before it as it sought freedom and justice. In this way, this community aspired to a notion of *prudentia*, or prudence.

Virtue also assumed the aspiration to a unified vision of life, a vision facilitated by the disciplined intellect and sharpened powers of discernment. Josef Pieper advises not to associate temperance too narrowly with *avoiding* excesses. *Temperare*, from whence "temperance" is derived, means to "dispose various parts into a unified and ordered whole."[22] With the help of evangelical Christianity and the ordered communality of the mutual aid and secret benevolent societies, African Americans were afforded the practical and theoretical foundation for life consistent with viability, the counterpart to the attempted contingency that racist society sought to impose on blacks. Through the call to virtuous living in the mutual aid society, the lodge hall, the church, and the home, an ordered and viable life could be enjoyed.

Bolstered by a vision for life that was ordered and shaped according to the dictates of prudence and temperance, the adherents of virtue among African Americans could assume a stance of boldness and courage as they fought against slavery and injustice. The viable life had to be lived and led in full independence of white racist oversight or control.

Frederick Douglass articulated this desired state of affairs in this way: "Independence is an essential condition of respectability. To be dependent, is to be degraded. Men may pity us, but they cannot respect us. We do not mean that we can become entirely independent of all men; that would be absurd and impossible in the social state. But we mean that we must become equally independent with other members of the Community."[23] The poignant desire of Henry Bibb to struggle against "external difficulties" as all free men are able to do captures this essence of fortitude.

Such courage, such boldness and tenacity, enabled these African American adherents of virtue to struggle for justice constantly and without equivocation. The aspiration toward this last virtue, the rightful distribution of power within U.S. society, was directed to abolishing slavery and granting full citizenship rights to black Americans. The energy to aspire toward this virtue, justice, proved to be the inevitable result of a disciplined intellect, nurtured within a context of an ordered life together.

These contexts for ordered life together—the mutual aid and secret societies in particular and the black community in general—urged blacks to be virtuous in demeanor and outlook, and sought to instill in their members the critical urgency for adhering to a virtuous life. Indeed, virtuous living and the survival of a people were deemed inseparable.

This book argues that efforts to attain viability in the African American community and the concomitant attempt to repel precariousness have found organizing power under the rubric of the pursuit of virtue. For African Americans, the pursuit of virtue has assisted in the quest to preserve and maintain a credible identity despite racist attempts to trivialize, demean, and deny the full humanity of black people. White racism has always sought to make blacks contingent beings. Moreover, white racism has always sought to destabilize the environment and social locations of black people in this country.

African Americans' quest for virtue has been a search for a meaningful place, a social location in which a sense of community could be forged. Their quest for virtue has been a principle for organizing life that emerges from the will to seek human wholeness in the face of historical and social realities attempting to negate such wholeness and render life contingent and precarious. It has been an effort among blacks to construct a degree of order—an inviolable sense of space—in the precarious and unstable situation that racist America sought to impose upon blacks. It has contributed to any identifiable organizing principle for African American survival in this country.

2

THE FIRST STIRRINGS

Ran away from the subscriber,
more than two years ago, a Negro man named Liberty. . . .
The fellow may have changed his name.

Raleigh Register, June 6, 1802

Puritan Seeds

The search for the historical roots of African American virtue takes us back to the time and world of the New England Puritans. In December 1693, Cotton Mather recorded in his diary a visit paid to him by a delegation of Boston slaves. The purpose of the visit, as Mather recalled it, was to seek his advice on ways to organize a "Meeting for the Welfare of their miserable Nation." Mather looked rather favorably on their petition and the purpose of their visit. He subsequently went to one of their homes to conduct prayer service and to preach from a passage that must have had special meaning to them: "Let Ethiopia hasten to stretch out its hands to God" (Ps. 68:31).

We can only surmise the thoughts that must have gone through the minds of the slaves upon hearing the words from which Mather preached; amidst the bondage in which they were being held by whites, here was a white cleric expounding on words suggesting special favor toward, and an implicit suggesting of, liberation from bondage. Indeed, the hope that Ethiopia's arms would be outstretched would surface repeatedly in later centuries as black Americans sought to forge a sense of identity and overthrow chains of oppression.

In his diary, Mather recorded the written pact that set forth the purposes of the association that the Boston slaves wished to form with his assistance. The document, subsequently printed as a flyer in 1706, was clearly the product of Mather's help and hand, even as it reflected the intentions of his visitors. The *Rules for the Society of Negroes* urged the members to meet for prayer services each Monday evening, being careful to secure the permission of their masters and to assemble between the hours of seven and nine so as not to be "unseasonably absent" from the families they served. Also, members promised to avoid all "wicked Company," receiving none into the fellowship who had not "sensibly reformed their Lives." Drunkenness, swearing, cursing, lying, and stealing were strictly forbidden. Those who committed such offenses were to be chastised and excluded from the association for one fortnight; in the case of fornication, after chastisement, the guilty party could be excluded for half a year; the person could be readmitted only if he gave "exemplary testimonies" of repentance and proof of "his becoming a new creature."[1]

Viewed closely in its totality, the document reveals an inherent tension that those blacks must have certainly felt. On the one hand, they were encouraged to practice a conventional Puritan piety, buttressed by the patronizing, albeit benevolent eye of a Cotton Mather. On the other hand, they must have felt the urge and intent to be sensitive to the welfare of other blacks. It is true that Mather condoned slavery and viewed Christianizing blacks as a method to make better servants. Yet he could argue forcefully in his treatise *The Negro Christianized* that blacks were not brutes and did possess souls.

Juxtaposed in the encounter between Mather and his visitors is in essence the conflict between goods—one set encouraged by Mather, acting in a way consistent with the aims of the slaveholding community of Puritans, and another set held dear by the same slaves who came to Mather for his peculiar wisdom on matters relating to religious communality. While the *Rules,* written and encouraged by Mather, could discourage aiding anyone who escaped from slavery, the members nevertheless pledged among themselves that they would "as wee have Opportunity, sett ourselves, to do all the good Wee can to the other Negro-Servants in the Town." And in each case where errant members committed moral offenses, the members pledged to do everything possible to redeem and "reclaim" such persons. Thus, within the very narrow confines of scrutiny by the Puritan white establishment, on the one hand, and the desire to live out a moral imperative with regard to other slaves, on the other, came the contours of virtue sought and expressed during the latter years of the seventeenth century.

The pursuit of this vision of virtue was necessarily constricted by the harsh realities of slavery to which blacks were bound. Given those realities, one should not be surprised to discern among blacks a deference to the white religious and civil authority that obviously countenanced such slavery. At the same time there was recorded—ironically, by the same hand that enjoined slaves to report escapes—an intense desire to show some clear regard for the moral and physical welfare of other slaves. Even within the strict confines of behavior expected within the slave regime, there was evident in the encounter with Cotton Mather an attempt among blacks to practice virtue.

But a much more vigorous articulation of the relationship between the aspiration toward virtue and human freedom lay ahead. The next stirring of the African American impulse toward the pursuit of virtue came forth as the young American nation was itself coming into being. The pursuit of virtue, as expressed during that period, was couched in much the same philosophical and moral claims that the colonists used to justify their revolt against the British crown, but was expressed in a desire to secure their freedom from slavery as well.

George Washington, in grieving over what appeared to be an inevitable conflict with Great Britain, surmised that "the once happy and peaceful plains of America are either to be drenched with Blood, or inhabited by Slaves." Washington was horrified at the prospect of white colonists reduced to a state of subservience to the British crown, a condition tantamount to living in a land "inhabited by Slaves." It was an intolerable situation. With distinct aversion to the prospect, he went on to ask, "Can a virtuous Man hesitate in his choice?"[2] Washington's choice was clear: he would not abide tyranny—or slavery—as, in his opinion, no virtuous man would.

Insofar as Washington and other colonists saw no contradiction between pressing claims for their freedom and denying it to Africans in their midst, the answer comes after carefully understanding the nuances of the political terms employed in the latter years of the eighteenth century. In an insightful study of rhetoric and public dis-

course relative to the word "equality" in American social consciousness, Condit and Lucaites remind us that within the context of eigh-
teenth-century Anglo-American political discourse, the word "equality" hardly held egalitarian connotations. "The British," they write,
"used the word 'liberty' to refer to a specific, balanced framework of
government." The colonists, in contrast, "dissatisfied with what the
British constitutional government delivered to them, began to treat
Liberty as a set of personal rights." Thus defined, the struggle for liberty could proceed in America side by side with the withholding of
liberty to others, especially if they were property. Or, as Condit and
Lucaites put it, "when the colonists explicitly proclaimed themselves
in favor of liberty and against slavery, they referred to *political,* not
chattel slavery."[3] Virtuous men of the new republic, rising in the
wilderness of America, were called upon to seek such liberty.

Washington would scarcely have understood why black people—135 of whom he held as slaves when he took to the field to
fight for his liberty and that of his compatriots—could stand on the
same principle of virtue as they would also come to demand freedom
from the same colonists who were insisting on their freedom from
the British crown. In 1773, a petition for freedom came from a
group of Massachusetts slaves to the royal governor, Thomas
Hutchinson. The slaves were well aware of the cruel anomaly that
prevailed at the time, which allowed some men to pledge their sacred
fortunes in the pursuit of their own freedom even while the same
men held others in bondage. The slaves could see clearly the political
issues at stake in their petition for freedom, but pressed their claims
mainly on moral and religious grounds.

Their petition was based on two premises: first, they, as well as
the ones who held them in bondage, were creatures of a God "who
is no respecter of persons"; and second, because they had attempted
to lead lives of virtue as successfully as most mortals could boast,
their enslavement constituted a moral outrage. Moreover, in their
case, they had adhered to virtuous living despite the enormity of the
obstacles that had been placed in their way. The slaves believed that
while their "condition is in itself so unfriendly to religion," they were
nevertheless "virtuous and religious, sober, honest and industrious."[4]

Based on such self-descriptions, it was a self-evident fact for them
that they did not deserve to be enslaved. The petition was also under-

girded by commonsense reasoning that all human beings were endowed with natural rights. Natural rights theory would form the foundation for the antislavery thought of Prince Hall, the father of black Freemasonry. Freed in 1770, Hall joined with seven other free blacks and petitioned the Massachusetts General Court to abolish slavery and restore the "Natural Right of all men." The petition was filed in 1777.

Two years later, a group of neighboring Connecticut slaves joined a belief in God with natural rights theory to demand freedom. A petition issued to the General Assembly of Connecticut in 1779 stated,

> Reason and Revelation join to declare, that we are the creatures of that God, who made of one blood, and Kindred, all the Nations of the Earth; we perceive by our own Reflection, that we are endowed with the same Faculties with our Masters, and there is nothing that leads us to a Belief, or Suspicion, that we are any more obliged to serve them, than they us, and the more we Consider of this matter, the more we are Convinced of our Right (by the Laws of Nature and by the whole Tenor of the Christian Religion, so far as we have been taught) to be free.[5]

In a similar fashion and in the fall of the same year, nineteen blacks in neighboring New Hampshire petitioned the House, meeting in Exeter, for freedom. Included among those blacks was Prince Whipple, who by some accounts had crossed the Delaware in the same boat with George Washington. The petitioners demanded their freedom "for the sake of justice, humanity, and the rights of mankind."[6] They argued that "the God of nature gave them life and freedom, upon the terms of the most perfect equality with other men; that freedom is an inherent right of the human species, not to be surrendered but by consent, for the sake of social life private or public. Tyranny and slavery are alike detestable to minds conscious of the equal dignity of human nature."

Even Phillis Wheatley, who is usually not associated with strong antislavery sentiment, could articulate within the context of her poetic allusions to the nature of virtue a decidedly vigorous protest against the institution. Her poetry had received enough critical acclaim that Benjamin Rush said in 1773 that her "singular genius and accomplishments are such as not only do honor to her sex but to human nature." That same year her volume *Poems on Various Subjects, Religious and Moral* was published in London. Although the total output of her literary labors did not devote a great deal of attention to slavery and the condition of other blacks, she did have a sense of outrage against slavery and a belief in the prominence of virtue within the moral universe, a universe in which slavery was a repugnant abomination. In July 1788 she wrote an elegiac poem, inspired by the death of General David Wooster. After praising the general and praying for the end of the war and a victory for the colonies, or "Columbia," she said,

> *But how presumptuous shall we hope to find*
> *Divine acceptance with the Almighty mind*
> *While yet o deed ungenerous they disgrace*
> *And hold in bondage Afric: blameless race*
> *Let virtue reign and then accord our prayers*
> *Be victory ours and generous freedom theirs.*[7]

Thus, Wheatley expressed a hope that the prominence of virtue within the civic fabric of the emerging new nation, the victorious "Columbia," would ensure the cessation of slavery and acceptance with the mind of almighty God.

Much earlier, in a letter to Rev. Samson Occum dated February 11, 1774, Wheatley affirmed the principle of the natural rights of human beings to be free, the mutual reinforcing support of civil and religious liberty, "which are so inseparably united." By her account, God has "implanted a Principle, which we call Love of Freedom; it is impatient of Oppression, and pants for Deliverance; and by the Leave of our modern Egyptians [slaveholders] I will assert that the same Principle lives in us."[8] This "implanted Principle" of which Wheatley wrote was affirmed as well by an ex-slave named Caesar Sarter who, in an essay published in 1774, noted the sanctity of natural rights.

In his discourse, Sarter recounted how he had been born free in Africa, had been captured and sold into slavery, and had labored in slavery for twenty years. As "Slavery is the greatest, and consequently most to be dreaded, of all temporal calamities; so its opposite, Liberty is the greatest temporal good with which you can be blest."[9]

Sarter questioned his reader thus: "Would you desire the preservation of your own liberty? As the first step let the oppressed Africans be liberated; then, and not till then, may you with confidence and consistency of conduct, look to Heaven for a blessing on your endeavours to knock the shackles with which your task masters are hampering you, from your own feet."

In addition to being grounded in natural rights theory, such appeals for freedom were critically linked to the appellants' vision of the virtuous life and their attempts to lead such a life. The Massachusetts slaves believed that while their "condition is in itself so unfriendly to religion," they were nevertheless "virtuous and religious, sober, honest and industrious." Implicit in the slave petitions was the belief that virtue and slavery were naturally incompatible. Coincidentally, during that period the prevailing natural rights theory, which was foundational to the American patriots' demand for political freedom from England, was appropriated by the slaves and others who would insist upon their freedom as well. To be sure, this insistence on freedom led them to a vigorous affirmation of the role of virtue in life—the free life—and virtue's incompatibility with slave life.

The Congregationalist cleric Lemuel Haynes powerfully articulated these ideas linking virtue and the early struggle for African American freedom. Haynes was born on July 18, 1753, the issue of a clandestine liaison between a black man and a white woman from a respectable family in West Hartford, Connecticut. Abandoned at the age of five months, he was taken into the household of a Congregationalist deacon, David Rose, and his family. Although he was legally an indentured servant, Haynes was raised as a virtual member of the family. At an early age he showed great facility in memorizing scriptures and sermons, and he freely absorbed the Calvinist theology of the deeply pious Rose household at regular household prayer gatherings. Freed from his bonds in 1774, and caught up in the Revolutionary fervor of the time, he enlisted as a minuteman. He saw active service in campaigns in the next year and at Fort Ticonderoga in 1776.

But Haynes's vocation in life would be the Christian ministry. After forgoing an opportunity to enter Dartmouth, in 1779 he decided to study Latin with a Connecticut minister who instructed him in exchange for farm labor. He became proficient in Greek through study with another minister, paying for his studies by serv-

ing as a schoolteacher. By 1780, Haynes was able to pass the scrutiny
of a board of ministerial examiners, which licensed him as a Congregational preacher. He was ordained in 1785 and three years later accepted the pastorate at a mainly white Congregational parish in
Rutland, Vermont, a post he would hold for more than thirty years.
In 1818 Haynes was dismissed from that church because of the combination of a surge in race prejudice and resentment over his pro-
Federalist political stance.[10] In the years before his death on September 28, 1833, he held other posts in Manchester, Vermont, and
Granville, New York.

Lemuel Haynes was a learned preacher and skilled orator, but
compared to other black clerics of the time, such as Richard Allen,
Peter Williams, and Absalom Jones, he was not known particularly
for outspokenness against slavery. He has not been remembered as
an oratorical firebrand in the service of the antislavery movement, although it is clear that he was familiar with the antislavery movement
and some of its leaders. For many who have studied his career, his
contributions to the antislavery movement in the context of his talents and the degree to which Providence smiled upon him reveal a
sense of disappointment. Many people have agreed with Vernon
Loggins, whose assessment of Haynes's work was summarized in this
terse statement: "If he had felt the scourge of slavery as strongly as he
felt the scourge of a Puritan God, he might, with all his talents, have
been an earlier Frederick Douglass."[11]

Yet in a manuscript by Haynes that lay hidden from scholars
until 1983, there is evidence that the black Puritan voiced a strong antislavery sentiment as early as 1776. His essay "Liberty Further
Extended: Or Free thoughts on the illegality of Slave-keeping," written the same year in which the Declaration of Independence was
penned, was a strident Revolutionary period antislavery tract as well as
a vision of the role of virtue in black people's demand for freedom.
Such a theme would echo some years later, in 1801, in a Fourth of
July sermon in which the renowned Congregationalist preacher of
color would ask, "On the whole does it not appear that a land of liberty is favourable to peace, happiness, virtue and religion, and should
be held sacred by mankind?"[12]

The sermonic essay of 1776 was written while Haynes was still
a member of the Rose household. There is some evidence that it was

a sermon that Haynes preached during one of the Sunday evening gatherings for friends and family members of the deeply religious, and apparently abolitionist, household. The essay betrays a rather inexperienced hand in matters of grammar, composition, and style; hence, it contrasts greatly with the facility and polish that Haynes would exhibit in his later sermons.

"Liberty Further Extended," despite its relative crudeness, sets forth perhaps the first statement from an African American in the sermonic essay form that attacked slavery. In his essay, Haynes's initial affirmations suggest that claims to liberty are couched in at least two foundational premises: first, in the presumption of natural rights— "Liberty, & freedom, is an innate principle, which is unmovebly placed in the human Species"—and second, within Christian theology as understood and embraced by Haynes. At other times these two foundations coalesce: "Liberty is a Jewel which was handed Down to man from the cabinet of heaven, and is Coaeval with his Existance." All men have equal rights to such liberty, even though some may "bost a superorety above another in point of Natural previledg." Such boasting was a "Lamantable consequence of the fall." Thus, Haynes thought it not "hyperbolical to affirm, that Even an affrican, has Equally as good a right to his Liberety in common with Englishmen." Moreover, Holy Scripture teaches that "it hath pleased god to make of one Blood all nations of men, for to dwell upon the face of the Earth" (Acts 17:26, KJV). Since every "privilege that mankind Enjoy have their Origen from god," the revocation of such a privilege by any other agent is rendered unjustifiable, lest the very nature of an immutable God be rendered false. In political and legal terms, "the practise of Slave-keeping, which so much abounds in this Land is illicit." According to natural rights theory and Christian theology, slavery is clearly wrong and unjustifiable.

For Haynes in his sermonic essay "Liberty Further Extended," slavery was inimical to what might be termed the purpose of human beings—implicitly, the living out of a virtuous life: "Men were made for more noble Ends than to be Drove to market, like Sheep and oxen." Moreover, slavery prevented its victims from exercising the moral prerogatives appertaining to parenthood. The children of slaves "are brought up under a partial Disapilne: their white masters haveing but Little, or no Effection for them. So that we may sup-

pose, that the abuses that they receive from the hands of their masters are often very consierable; their parents Being placed in such a
Situation as not being able to perform relative Deutys." Such are
those restrictions they are kept under "By their task-mastrs that they
are render'd incapable of performing theor morral Deutys Either to
God or man that are infinitely binding on all the human race."

More than twenty years later, in an 1801 Fourth of July sermon, Haynes suggested that there exists a mutually inimical relationship between slavery and true virtue. Slavery attempts to destroy
a sense of self-worth, without which the practice or conception of
virtue is impossible. In slavery, Haynes asserted, blacks have been
taught to view themselves as a "rank of beings far below others,
which has suppressed, in a degree, every principle of manhood, and
so they become despised, ignorant and licentious."[13]

Virtue is a natural ingredient of the free life; it is the necessary
characteristic of free persons. Therefore the continued enslavement
of those who would aspire to virtue is an unnatural act in the moral
universe of the slaves. A slave petition issued in Massachusetts in
1774 went so far as to assert that "we cannot serve our God as we
ought whilst in this situation."[14] The presumed natural incompatibility between slavery and virtue, between slave existence and the virtuous free life, was echoed years later by an anonymous "free Negro"
who reminisced about his former life as a slave. "The condition of
the slave is," he recalled, "nothing more deplorable than in its being
so unfavorable to the practice of every virtue."[15]

The early stirrings of a notion of virtue among black people undergirded demands for freedom, both in individual cases and in the
general demand that slavery cease as a practice in the country that was
itself demanding political freedom from the English crown. The petitions were obviously directed toward the political establishment at
large. But there emerged as well another mode of presentation of such
notions of virtue and directed more to the black community itself.

A curious and notable genre of early African American literature emerged from the northern black community toward the latter
years of the eighteenth century and served as a poignant vehicle to
project the idea of virtue and virtuous living. Essentially, this genre
amounted to what I have chosen to call "the confessions of the
doomed man." The writings consisted of the recorded last words of

persons sentenced to death for certain crimes, the prescribed punishment for which appears rather harsh to modern sensibilities; men mounted the gallows for such crimes as burglary or horse thievery in those days. The last words of the condemned were arranged in such a way by his confessor that they became a powerful exhortation to members of the black community to lead lives of piety and virtue—lest they meet the same fate as the condemned.

For example, Johnson Green's *Life and Confession* began with this typical, yet moving opening statement: "I, Johnson Green, having brought myself to a shameful and ignominious death by my wicked conduct and, as I am a dying man, I leave to the world the following History of my Birth, Education, and vicious Practices hoping that all people will take warning by my evil example and shun vice and follow virtue."[16] Green went on to give an incredibly detailed account of his life of petty crime, which he began at an early age, and which culminated in the "atrocious crime of burglary" for which he was convicted and sentenced to hang on August 17, 1786. Born of a black father and an Irish mother, he began stealing at the age of twelve—"four cakes of gingerbread and six biscuits out of a horse cart." Green served in the Continental Army, and while stationed at West Point in 1781 he and two other soldiers broke open a sutler's "markee" and stole "three cheeses, one small fiskin of butter and some chocolate." His punishment was one hundred lashes. Unrepentant and undeterred, he resumed a life of petty thievery, going to Rhode Island in 1784, returning to Massachusetts, and being convicted in Worcester for burglary two years later.[17] He summed up his lamentable tale of misdeeds with these words:

> Thus have I given a history of my birth, education and atrocious conduct, and as the time is very nigh in which I must suffer an ignominious death, I earnestly intreat [*sic*] that all people would take warning by my wicked example; that they would shun the paths of destruction by guarding against every temptation; that they would shun vice, follow virtue, and become (through the assistance of the Almighty) victorious over the enemies of immortal felicity, who are exerting themselves to delude and lead nations to destruction.

It is likely that "confessions" of this sort reflected a literary talent that far exceeded the gifts of repentant, but no doubt illiterate, persons such as Johnson Green. These confessions bear a strong editorial influence of a pious bent. There is good reason to believe that pious persons, perhaps clergymen, were involved in recording and disseminating these confessions to the general public.

One such confession that has been preserved bears the marked influence of Richard Allen, the chief founder of the African Methodist Episcopal Church. John Joyce, a convicted murderer, was accompanied to the gallows on March 14, 1808, by Allen, three other clergy, and one layman. Most likely after hearing Joyce's confession, Allen recorded the man's words in his own stylistic fashion. It is a fact that just before Joyce's execution the confessions were in Allen's possession; he had them duly registered two years later on March 10, 1810, in Philadelphia under a formal title: "Confession of John Joyce, alias Davis, who was executed on Monday, the 14th of March, 1808, for the Murder of Mrs. Sarah Cross, with an address to the public and people of colour, together with the substance of the trial and the address of Chief Justice Tilghman, on his condemnation." With a note of somber irony, the document had been registered in conformity with an act of Congress entitled "An Act for the encouragement of learning." In this way, then, the condemned man became a grim tutor in virtue's schoolhouse.

The method of inculcating public moral education through the confessions of the doomed man had all the strengths and limitations of a system of moral education that was based on fear. These confessions were exercises in negative reinforcement; they literally sought to frighten the black community into compliance with virtuous living. And they surely reinforced the popular racism of the time, which always tended to hold blacks up in stereotypical fashion. Indeed, the vast majority of editions published in the colonies between 1675 and 1800 dealing with black individuals were devoted to those with criminal pasts.[18] However, it has been argued that at least these narratives, despite their tendency to vaunt less than flattering popular images of blacks, accorded the protagonists in them "an assertion of humanity." In them, one literary critic has asserted, "the narrators take responsibility for their actions, thus indicating a sense of themselves as persons with some degree of self-determination."[19]

Virtue and Mutual Aid

There was yet another context in which the early stirrings for a notion of virtue among African Americans developed. The call for virtuous living was also powerfully reinforced in the early mutual aid societies that emerged among free blacks during the Revolutionary War period. The early mutual aid societies helped free blacks in urban communities find financial assistance in personal and family crises.

While it was clear that prior to the War of Independence some colonies had abolished slavery or were on the road to doing so, it was not clear that the status of blacks was such that they were accorded full inclusion in the social, economic, and cultural life of the emerging nation. Among the free blacks in the North, life could be a frustrating and seemingly hopeless morass of socially constricted opportunities for living fully. Discriminatory hiring practices meant that black people were relegated for the most part to the semiskilled and menial positions in the economy. No "safety net" of public resources was available for destitute and economically marginal blacks. Thus, black people had to look within the resources of their own community to mitigate the economic precariousness that white antipathy caused. The response within the black community was the development of mutual aid societies. Such societies were in essence associations formed to afford their members material assistance in case of need.

Perhaps the earliest formally organized mutual aid society among black Americans was the African Union Society, formed in 1780 in Newport, Rhode Island, by a man named Newport Gardner and some friends.[20] This mutual aid society would set a pattern for ones to come in that it would be more than merely an economic institution: it would provide for cultural, educational, and spiritual needs of its members as well. It could be argued that the African Union Society actually functioned as a quasi-church. It recorded births, marriages, and deaths and provided for Christian burials. The society's informal religious function became more formalized when, in 1824, it spawned the first black church in Newport. It furthered its educational goals by merging with the African Benevolent Society to establish a free school for black children in 1807. This interplay between the religious, educational, and associational aspects of the black community was fairly common, although in some instances the mutual aid society and the school followed, and were outgrowths of, the church and its activities.[21]

Within the same decade as the founding of the African Union Society of Newport came the momentous birth of the Free African Society in Philadelphia under the leadership of Richard Allen and Absalom Jones in the spring of 1787. Allen and Jones were part of a dynamic vanguard of black preachers (including Peter Williams in New York; David George, Andrew Bryan, and George Liele in South Carolina and Georgia) whose organizing efforts resulted in what is now known as the independent black movement of the latter part of the eighteenth century, a movement that sought religious autonomy from patronizing and oppressive white oversight. Both Allen and Jones were born in slavery, Allen in Philadelphia in 1760, Jones in Sussex, Delaware, in 1746. In 1777 Allen was converted to Methodism. About the same time, his master was so moved by a sermon preached by a Methodist circuit preacher, Rev. Freeborn Garrettson, that he offered Allen and his brother a chance to purchase their freedom. Garrettson had liberated his own slaves in 1775. Allen and his brother were able to purchase their freedom for sixty pounds, or two thousand dollars in inflated Continental currency.

Allen then went on to support himself by cutting wood and transporting salt in a circuit that took him from Delaware through New Jersey to Pennsylvania. Along the way he would preach as well, mostly to whites, who were impressed mightily by the force of his presentation. It is likely that Allen was present at the first organizing conference of American Methodism when it met in December of 1784 in Baltimore.[22] His preaching and personal charisma were of such profundity that Bishop Francis Asbury, the English apostle of American Methodism, asked Allen to accompany him on his preaching forays into the southern slave states. Allen declined the offer since it was laden with the condition that he not mix with slaves he would encounter along the way. Instead Allen continued preaching on his own until at last he was summoned in February of 1786 to come to St. George's Methodist Episcopal Church in Philadelphia to minister principally to the blacks who were worshiping in that congregation. There he would meet Absalom Jones.

As a sixteen-year-old slave, Jones had been brought to Philadelphia in 1762 to be put to work in a shop. There a clerk taught him to read and write, and in 1766 he was permitted to study in night school. Four years later, he married one of his master's slaves and bought her freedom with money they earned working evenings for wages. Industrious and energetic, they soon were able to acquire a home and other property, and the greatest boon—his eventual freedom in 1784. By the time Richard Allen came to Philadelphia in 1786, Jones had become a prominent member among the blacks at St. George's Methodist Episcopal Church.

Although St. George's was a racially mixed congregation, it was anything but hospitable to its black members. Allen had been engaged to minister primarily to the blacks, yet he was assigned the improbable hour of five o'clock in the morning at which to preach. Allen preached at that hour but considered it a "great cross to bear."[23] Other indignities abounded. Black congregants were forced to sit in separate sections of the church; they could receive communion only after white congregants had been served. Expectedly, the blacks within the congregation began to chafe under such unkind treatment at the hands of their ostensible Christian brothers and sisters and sought ways in which they could exercise more religious autonomy.

The irony is that in an effort to secure a greater measure of religious freedom, and the vision of building a separate edifice for them, the critical step Allen, Jones, and others took was to form a secular mutual aid society. This society, the Free African Society, came into being in May of 1787. While religious and spiritual matters were always important to those who formed the group, mutual aid and support for the weak were equally major concerns of the members. In its preamble the members of the society exulted, "We the free Africans and their descendants . . . do unanimously agree, for the benefit of each other."

But the provision of help available in the mutual aid society came with a price: the strict adherence to a regimen of upright behavior. If the mutual aid society could be counted upon to provide assistance in times of distress, it expected its members to walk at all times in paths of strict rectitude. The preamble of the Free African Society of Philadelphia would welcome members into that association "provided the persons lived an orderly and sober life." The New York African Clarkson Society, named after the great English antislavery proponent Thomas Clarkson, desired as members only "free persons of moral character."[24] In the African Society of Boston, for example, a widow of a deceased member could receive benefits as long as "she behaves herself decently" and—in deference to the fiscal integrity of the group—"remains a widow."[25] The Brotherly Union Society was even more severe in its expectations of moral behavior of persons who received benefits: any member who fraudulently received benefits or "spent his time in brothels, or in gambling or in tippling shops" would be expelled immediately.

Despite the clear pronouncements from these groups on the importance of personal piety, an analysis of the ethical import of these early mutual aid societies reveals that the emphasis on personal rectitude did not imply that these societies were devoid of a consciousness of the corporate nature of morality or of the belief that virtue in and of itself was a good to be pursued. There was the implicit assertion that personal morality should motivate one to participate actively in the welfare of the group, especially for the good of less fortunate persons. Thus, within the economic function of the mutual aid society lay an essential ethical imperative: mutual aid by definition required at some point that each individual be prepared to offer substantive aid to others.

Yet the tenor and attitudes of these societies went quite beyond the offering of monetary aid to the financially needy. The overall welfare of the society at large, its moral, spiritual, and intellectual aspects, was also a concern of mutual aid societies. They sought to uplift the whole person. There was the affirmation that wherever true personal piety existed, it could not help manifesting itself as an integral part of the wider social context.

Prince Saunders, in addressing the Pennsylvania Augustine Society, spoke of this link between personal piety and social context: "Wherever these lofty and commending views of piety and virtue have been encouraged, a high sense of the social, moral and practical obligations and duties of life have been cherished and cultivated with an elevated and an invincible zeal."[26] Because the Afric-American Female Intelligence Society of Boston felt itself to be "actuated by a natural feeling for the welfare of our friends," the women "thought fit to associate for the diffusion of knowledge, the suppression of vice and immorality, and for cherishing such virtues as will render us happy and useful to society."[27] A sense of the social or corporate context was prominent in the preamble of the African Society of Boston when the members affirmed that they would "watch over each other in their spiritual concerns; and by advice, exhortation, and prayer excite each other to grow in Grace, and in the Knowledge of our Lord and Savior Jesus Christ, and to live soberly, righteously, and Godly in this present world, that we may all be accepted of the Redeemer, and live together with him in Glory hereafter."[28]

The spiritual essence of corporate concern was further articulated by William Hamilton, a noted early-nineteenth-century antislavery spokesman and a member of the African Society of New York. In an address before the other members he reminded them that "mere socialities [sic] is not the object of our formation, but to improve the mind, soften the couch of the sick, to administer an elixir to the afflicted, to befriend the widow, and become the orphan's guardian." Asked Hamilton, "Is this not a noble employment, can there be found a better; you ought to be proud to be engaged in such an exercise. It is employment of this kind that raises the man up to the emperium, or the highest heaven."[29] Participation in the corporate dimensions and needs of the group was, therefore, perceived as spiritual enterprise, a quest for true virtue.

Thus, these early mutual aid societies were not only associations designed to mitigate economic hardship for members, but were also contexts in which the wider societal uses of virtue and virtuous pursuits could be encouraged. The mutual aid society and the moral climate that it fostered also laid the groundwork for a belief that the path to virtue could be pursued from a more positive stance, a belief that moral sensibility could be developed through the pursuit of a positive ideal rather than through the avoidance of punishment or deprivation of desired goods. Such visions of the good have values in and of themselves.

Prince Hall, the recognized founder of Masonic lodges among black Americans, preached a Masonic sermon to his brothers in the lodge on June 24, 1797, and articulated this vision: "Now my brethren, nothing is stable, all things are changeable. Let us seek those things which are sure and steadfast, and let us pray God that, while we remain here, he would give us the grace of patience and strength to bear up under all our troubles, which, at the day, God knows, we have our share of."[30] Even in the same sternly puritanical mutual aid societies there was a hint of the suggestion that virtue's natural sibling was not the avoidance of punishment but the eager desire to be a social good or to do something socially useful.

Moreover, this attempt to inculcate virtue from such a stance was developed precisely within the context of a very real hope for the end of slavery, the willingness to struggle for freedom and to work for the eventual political and economic empowerment of all African Americans. That great moral good was linked with the pursuit of virtue. After all, if the implicit message in the early slave petitions was that slave existence and the pursuit of true virtue were inimical to each other, then the fight against slavery was a natural consequence of such thought. Following the logic of their understanding of virtue, many African American thinkers would be drawn ineluctably to the struggle against the vice of slavery.

Celebrating Freedom's First Glimmer

On March 2, 1807, Congress passed a law that, when it took effect nine months later, prohibited the further importation of African slaves into the United States. Although there might have been reason for jubilance among the antislavery forces and the black community, the actual effects of the law were less than salutary. Its enforcement would prove to be so erratic that for years thereafter, slave ships could still ply the waters off U.S. ports with near impunity, bringing in their cargoes of African captives. Yet the day on which the law took effect, January 1, 1808, was nevertheless a significant one for people who looked for any signs of the eventual abolition of slavery in the United States. On that very day Peter Williams delivered an oration in the African Church in New York commemorating the abolition of the trade, and looked forward to the day when slavery itself would cease and the time speedily come when "Ethiopia shall stretch forth her hand; when the sun of liberty shall beam resplendent on the whole African race," and when, Williams continued, "its genial influences promote the luxuriant growth and knowledge of virtue."[31] On that very same day as well, the venerable Absalom Jones mounted the pulpit of St. Thomas's African Episcopal Church in Philadelphia to lead a celebration of the end of the slave trade. Recounting the story of the liberation of the Hebrew slaves, Jones assured his audience that "the deliverance of the children of Israel from their bondage is not the only instance in which it has pleased God to appear in behalf of oppressed and distressed nations."[32] He went on to assert that the "great and blessed event, which we have this day met to celebrate, is a striking proof that the God of heaven and earth is *the same, yesterday, and today, and forever*" (Jones's emphasis). Even an orator of more philosophical bent, such as Russell Parrott, could affirm that the very idea of an essentially moral universe meant that the evil of slavery had to end. Before an audience in 1814, Parrott explained that the demise of slavery constituted "a sacrifice that virtue compelled avarice to make."³³ Yet, to be sure, virtually all the public speakers of this era affirmed that the glimmer of freedom, which the end of the slave trade betokened, was a light that God had ignited. Since it was therefore apparent to these celebrants of the abolition of the slave trade that God had put in place an inevitable series of historical events that would culminate in freedom, an orator like Joseph Sidney would not think it presumptuous to "look forward to the period when slavery, in this land of freedom, will be unheard of and unknown."³⁴

The celebrations throughout the black communities of the North on the occasion of the abolition of the slave trade, and on successive anniversaries, became events when those communities could be reminded of the bitter experiences of other blacks who were still in chains in the South. Moreover, northern free blacks could remember on those occasions their efforts to secure a greater measure of freedom for the race and to express in a corporate setting their fervent hope for the eventual end of slavery in the United States. Each occasion was in essence a worship event in which a kind of sacred history and story of promise could be recounted for the faithful.

The Rev. Paul Dean, minister of Boston's First Universal Church, although apparently white, told such a story as the invited guest speaker of the African Society of Boston as they celebrated an anniversary in 1819. There is reason to believe that Dean struck a resonant chord among his listeners when he declared that slavery, "with an unhallowed hand," had "robbed the sons and daughters of Jehovah of their liberty; and with an unpitying eye seen them writhe and smart beneath the lash." Dean went on to assert that the abolition of the slave trade was an indication that slavery's "power is broken. . . . [Its] sceptre is shortened . . . and [its] terrors are fast diminishing." Slavery will end, most assuredly for Dean, because "the Son of God, moved with compassion, hath graciously espoused the cause of the oppressed, and never, never will he forsake it, till a most glorious jubilee shall declare every man to be free."³⁵

The exhortations on such occasions were also meant to encourage members of the free black community to ponder the implications of their freedom, the disparity between the condition of their enslaved brothers and sisters in the South and their own. We have already seen how an implicit assertion among some slave petitions was that virtue could best be pursued and cultivated within the context of the free life. This belief was lent credence within African American consciousness as it manifested itself among free blacks. Those blacks understood their freedom as integrally tied to the pursuit of the cultivation of virtue. When slavery was abolished in New York in 1827, Rev. Nathaniel Paul asked an audience at a July 5 celebration, "What is liberty without virtue . . . and what is freedom but a curse, and even destruction, to the profligate?"[36] Paul Dean asserted before his hearers, as they rejoiced in their freedom, "For in the same proportion that God multiplies your blessings and privileges, he also increases your duty and responsibility. Your privileges, good as they are, if they are not improved, will not only cease to be such, but will leave upon your hands an awful responsibility for not having improved them."

Essentially then, celebrative events became occasions on which a sacred history could be recounted and the hope for the fully free and fully virtuous life of every member of the African American community could be contemplated. On January 1, 1813, five years after the abolition of the slave trade, Rev. George Lawrence stood in the pulpit of New York's African Methodist Episcopal Church and delivered an oration that sought to put this historical event in the proper moral perspective for his hearers. Eventually published as a pamphlet in the same year, the oration was prefaced by remarks that set the tone of heightened group consciousness and duty as a moral good. In the introductory remarks, Peter Malachi Eagans wrote, "I have from my earliest youth rejoiced in the felicity of my fellow men, and have ever considered it as an indispensable duty of every member of society to promote as far as in him lies the prosperity of every individual, but *more especially of the community to which he belongs.*"[37]

In assessing the continuing tragedy that enslaved so many blacks in the South, Lawrence advised that the clear goal for all blacks should be unity, for "the glory of a people is union; united in the bonds of social love, they become strong and vigorous, wise and discerning." For Lawrence, the virtue that engenders this union is love. Love, transformed into social power and force, can have dramatic consequences, for "without it no quality of heart, no action of life is valuable in itself, or pleasing to God." Love as the basis for a rallying point will ward against "animosities and contentions" within the African American community but will also "bring down the blessings of heaven upon our heads." Moreover, the unifying power of this love unleashed will "slay our enemies and make alive our friends—and shall cause our society to flourish, and this shall break the chain that still holds thousands of our brethren in bondage."[38]

Lawrence was rather unclear about exactly how love would "slay our enemies." Perhaps it was just so much powerful rhetoric designed to instill in the hearers the energy to do what the words themselves could not do. And yet one discerns upon further reading of his "Oration" that the outward appearance of virtue could have a discernibly strategic value. Using metaphoric language and images, Lawrence asserted the power he believed a virtuous example could have: "As the continual dropping of water has a tendency to wear away the hardest and most flinty substance, so likewise shall we, abounding in good works, and causing our examples to shine forth as the sun at noon day, meet their callous hearts, and render sinewless the arm of sore oppression."[39] Victory is forthcoming to such persons who "cling closely to the paths of virtue and morality, who cherish the plants of peace and temperance." By being "zealous and vigilant," by always being "alert to promote the welfare of your injured brethren," Lawrence assured his listeners that Providence would "shower down her blessings upon your heads and crown your labors with success."

At the end of the eighteenth century and the first years of the nineteenth, the first stirrings of a unique conception of virtue among African Americans had begun to emerge and take shape. This conception of virtue would flourish and develop even further as African Americans would seek to galvanize their efforts in the formal and political struggle against slavery, a struggle that claimed not only the physical energy of black people but their intellectual acuity as well. We now turn to the years of this struggle.

3

AFRICAN AMERICAN STRUGGLE

AND THE

FORGING OF FOUR VIRTUES

First, my young friends, let me invite you to the path of virtue.

Oration by William Hamilton

commemorating the abolition of slavery in

New York State, July 5, 1827

LONG BEFORE THE SHOTS that began the Civil War were fired, African Americans were obliged to fight an earlier war with no less vigor and intensity than the one their descendants would fight years later in places such as Fort Pillow, Fort Wagner, and Petersburg. At the beginning of the nineteenth century white people in the United States by and large, in print and in publicly sanctioned discourse, seemed to share a consensus that black people constituted an alien and unassimilable element in the population.[1]

Despite a legal system that upheld slavery and the pervasive cultural patterns that sanctioned a diminished political status of free blacks, many African Americans still believed they had a place in the destiny of the United States. In the early part of the nineteenth century, as black people sought to counter notions held by the vast majority of Americans that no viable place could be found for them in this country, they found within the idea of virtue a means with which they believed they could repulse any denigration of their humanity. The idea of virtue became the quarry from which black abolitionists would mine an array of weapons for use against the prevalent racism and against the institution of slavery. Virtue's pursuit in the context of countering racism became the major goal toward which they would harness the power of pen, pulpit, and personal sacrifice. This chapter will discuss how the African American conception of virtue came of age in the first half of the nineteenth century as blacks fought against oppression and sought to gain a full measure of race integrity and uplift.

We have already defined the African American conception of virtue as a vision of a divinely ordered life in which the disciplined intellect enables persons to struggle against injustice and to forge communities and structures that could ensure the development of the furthest moral and material possibilities of African Americans. Prudence, temperance, fortitude, and justice—the cardinal virtues—took on new and urgent meaning in the minds and strivings of the black exponents of virtue. They would understand that prudence, or wisdom, would have to be applied to the actual and frightful conditions that confronted people of color. Temperance would be more than mere pretensions to piety and the avoidance of vice; temperance would connote a comprehensive vision of personal and corporate rectitude that could be foundational for the moral as well as the material well-being of black people. Courage, or fortitude, would be understood as a necessary characteristic for anyone involved in the struggle against those who held enormous power. Finally, their quest for justice envisioned equitable relations among people and a building of a just state that would not only abolish slavery but also ensure that the power of the people would prevail in a truly *republican* form of government.

Prudence and the African American Quest for the Enlightened Mind

Racist ideology and popularly held conceptions of Africans and blacks presumed the natural intellectual superiority of whites and the corresponding inferiority of blacks. Such a presumption was clearly useful as a justification for the enslavement of Africans and the continued dominance of whites over American blacks, slave and free. This presumption of the basic intellectual inferiority of blacks enraged black thinkers and forced them to cultivate a near obsession with the quest to cultivate their minds and to build contexts among them that could nourish and enrich the mind. In response to racist ideology, African American proponents of virtue championed the efficacy and power of the disciplined intellect, not only as a refutation of notions of black inferiority but as a way of ordering reality so that a sustained and confident fight against oppression could be waged. In so doing these thinkers affirmed prudence as an aspect of virtue.

The eventual end to which the disciplined intellect would be directed was of a decidedly pragmatic nature. The extolling of the power and beauty of the human mind for the African American proponents of virtue would be more than the celebration of speculative thought; it would constitute an affirmation of the disciplined mind to provide a basis by which they could negotiate their way through the perilous waters of an often hostile U.S. social system. Prudence for them would be very much reminiscent of the classical virtue of prudence, or "the practical expression of wisdom."[2] Such wisdom, as opposed to theoretical wisdom, would be able to provide the resources for "ordering means of the rational achievement of goals" in life.[3]

Perhaps the most incendiary piece of writing to come from the pen of a black man during the first third of the nineteenth century was David Walker's *Appeal in Four Articles*, published in 1829. Within the four arguments that constituted the work was the affirmation that knowledge and the development of the intellect would be key factors in the ultimate destruction of slavery and the building of integrity in African American life.

Walker was born on September 28, 1785, in Wilmington, North Carolina. His father, who was a slave, died before his birth, and Walker was brought up, without learning to read and write, by his mother, a free woman. Experiencing all of the contempt with which slaveholding society held free blacks, he determined at some point in his youth to leave North Carolina. His words give ample testimony to his hatred of his circumstances:

> If I remain in this bloody land, I will not live long. As true as God reigns, I will be avenged for the sorrow which my people have suffered. This is not the place for me—no, no. I must leave this part of the country. It will be a great trial for me to live on the same soil where so many men are in

slavery; certainly I cannot remain where I must hear chains continually, and where I must encounter the insults of their hypocritical enslavers. Go, I must.[4]

By 1825 he had moved to Boston, and two years later set up a secondhand clothing business, which he managed with moderate success. By 1828 he was prosperous enough to marry, also having become a vocal and visible leader among Boston's blacks, speaking out publicly on the necessity for black unity and against the complacency he perceived in some quarters of the black community.

With the publication of the *Appeal* in September 1829, he gained instant notoriety. His blistering and unequivocal attack on slavery was so strong that even some of the most advanced abolitionists turned against him. Benjamin Lundy said of the *Appeal*: "A more bold, daring, inflammatory publication, perhaps, never issued from the press of any country. I can do no less than set the broadest seal of condemnation on it. Such things can have no effect than to injure our cause."[5] Walker was determined, however, to speak as a black man, unfettered by even well-meaning white abolitionists. The *Appeal* was met with outrage in the South. The governor of Georgia wrote the mayor of Boston, requesting him to suppress it. The mayor replied that he had "no power nor disposition" to do so.[6] With a price of one thousand dollars on his head, ten times that if taken alive, Walker refused the entreaties of friends to flee to Canada. Said he, "I will stand my ground. Somebody must die in this cause." Indeed, one year after the publication of his *Appeal*, at the age of thirty-four, Walker died under mysterious circumstances. There can be little doubt that the *Appeal*, and the notoriety it caused, led to his death.

Consisting of four articles, the *Appeal* looked into the causes of the "wretchedness" and dire circumstances of blacks. Walker determined that slavery, the hypocrisy of organized religion, the racism undergirding colonization schemes, and ignorance were the chief causes of the misery of the black community.

To counter what he perceived to be a depressing level of ignorance in the black community, Walker proposed a turning toward enlightenment as a way of living in the world so that the "happiness" of black people could be assured. Moreover, he envisioned a kind of moral education that prepared people to act in ways consistent with black freedom. Citing an "ignorant" black woman who had senselessly aided in the recapture of escaped slaves, Walker called upon his brethren and sisters "to cast your eyes upon the wretchedness of your brethren and to do your utmost to enlighten them" by "doing what you can to rescue them and yourselves from degradation." Walker hoped that enlightened black people would bestir themselves to work for the "entire emancipation of your enslaved brethren all over the world, for I believe that it is the will of the Lord that our greatest happiness shall consist in working for the salvation of our whole body."[7] Moral education as understood by David Walker entailed action and a way of life in which persons would be able to discern rightly the peculiar interests of black people and order their lives accordingly.

While he understood the critical importance of formal education, he also appreciated the ability to put formal education into practical use. He lamented a conversation with a black man who boasted of his son's penmanship, claiming that he could "write as well any white man," but who, when pressed about his son's knowledge of grammar and geography and his ability to post accounts in an acceptable manner, conceded the boy's inability to do so. Walker thus decried superficial education, praying "that the Lord might undeceive [sic] my ignorant brethren, and permit them to throw away pretensions, and seek after the substance of learning."[8]

Another tireless activist and lecturer in the cause of abolition and black uplift was the notable Maria Stewart. Her life and thought are obvious exemplars of the importance of the enlightened intellect in the cause of justice and black integrity. Along with Walker and many others, she exemplified those who could articulate the significance of virtue within the context of social action. Born free in Hartford, Connecticut, in 1803, Maria Stewart became a vigorous lecturer and activist in the reform, temperance, and abolitionist movements. She saw no inconsistency in working for all of those efforts, for in her mind slavery, intemperance, and other sins were all cut from the same perverse cloth. She believed that there was a dire need for moral reform in U.S. society and attributed those moral transgressions to a general lack of virtue within that society.

Maria Stewart was five years old when she was orphaned and subsequently bound out to a Congregational clergyman's home as a servant. Most likely in the environment of that home she had "the seeds of piety and virtue sown in [her] mind," but did not wish that such piety would place undue constraints on her curiosity about the world around her. She coveted a liberal education at an early age. Primarily through her inquisitiveness and resourcefulness, she acquired the rudiments of such an education, supplemented by attending Sunday schools from the time she was fifteen years of age until she was twenty. In 1826 she married James W. Stewart, a veteran of the War of 1812, but was widowed three short years later. She was left impoverished after unscrupulous lawyers cheated her out of her widow's inheritance.

Because abolitionists recognized her natural oratorical gifts, she was put on the lecture circuit and thereby derived the means of a livelihood, modest as it was. Six of her speeches became the basis for her work *The Productions of Mrs. Maria W. Stewart.* Included in this work were many meditations, mostly based on the Psalms. William Lloyd Garrison published many of her speeches in the *Liberator,* and her fame as an abolitionist lecturer spread far and wide.

Simultaneous with joining the abolitionist cause, Stewart had a profound religious experience in 1830. Through that experience she was brought to "the knowledge of the truth, as it is in Jesus," culminating in a "public profession of . . . faith in Christ" in 1831. The intense religious experience fired her activism and thought to promote ideas such as the centrality of the virtuous life, the pursuit of righteousness, and the acquisition of knowledge as crucial components in the process of the liberation of blacks and uplift of the race. After her experience she wrote, "From the moment I experienced the change [conversion], I felt a strong desire, with the help and assistance of God, to devote the remainder of my days to piety and virtue, and now possess the spirit of independence that, were I called upon, I would willingly sacrifice my life for the cause of God and my brethren."[9]

On the importance of knowledge and its crucial role in the virtuous life, she was insistent. In what might have been one of her earliest speeches, given at the African Masonic Hall in Boston in 1833, she expressed her belief in the exercise of acquiring knowledge and intellectual nurturing as components of the life of virtue. The attempt of racist society to deny humanity to blacks, the fact that blacks were "looked upon as objects of pity and commiseration [has] filled my soul with a holy indignation, and compelled me thus to come forward, and endeavor to turn their attention to knowledge and improvement," adding defiantly, "for knowledge is power."[10]

African American thinkers who pursued the idea of virtue firmly believed that a universal moral order undergirded the world and that human beings were endowed with a capacity to understand that order and to act responsibly in it. Speaking before the Humane Mechanics Society, Rev. Joseph Corr, for example, commended to other members of the society "the practice of virtue; that unchanging principle of heavenly origin."[11] Although virtue has a divine origin, its effects are destined to be of distinct value to human life, promoting "true happiness and true enjoyment." Because Corr believed "the human mind is the direct image of God," he could affirm that the "rational desire of all intelligent beings" was consistent with and in "accordance with the mandates of the Great Sovereign of the universe." This endowment of the "noble faculty of reason" produces in humanity a "restless desire for the acquirement of knowledge."[12]

The type of knowledge desired, however, would enable persons to make significant changes in their environment. What was desired was prudence, the ability to discern the order of reality and act upon it and to change that reality if necessary. According to the logic of their pursuit of virtue, prudence was precisely the intellectual tool needed to mount a sustained battle against real evils in the world, the most noxious being the continuance of chattel slavery. Moreover, the presumption of such powers on their part would constitute a powerful rebuke to holders of racist theories who believed that black people were not capable of rational thought or did not possess strength of character to be able to effect substantial change in the world. They also understood that education would be critically important as they sought to counter the attempts of U.S. culture to render them contingent and powerless.

The Negro Convention Movement

The belief in the inherent order of the moral universe and the hope that a sharpened intellect could help shape human society in conformity with such a universe were given organizational focus in the work of the Negro convention movement and its offshoot, the American Moral Reform Society, both of which flourished in the 1830s. The convention movement was perhaps the principal national forum in which free blacks could articulate and debate their views on the major issues of the day that affected the destiny of African Americans.

At the call of Richard Allen and Hezekiah Grice, a Baltimore ice dealer, forty African Americans came to Philadelphia on September 15, 1830, to meet at Allen's Bethel African Methodist Episcopal Church, the mother church of the A.M.E. denomination. Because of the threat of mob violence, the group was forced to meet in secret, but decided to hold public meetings, come what may, from September 20 to 24. Richard Allen was chosen president of this first convention.

That the virtuous life, the pursuits of the mind, and race uplift were perceived to be inextricably bound together is clear from the proceedings of what would come to be called the First Convention of Free Persons of Colour. In a corporate address to the convention, Bishop Allen and others affirmed a key relationship between mental preparedness and economic stability: "That our mental and physical qualities have not been more actively engaged in pursuits more lasting, is attributable in a great measure to a want of unity among ourselves; whilst our only stimulus to action has been to become domestics, which at best is but a precarious and degrading situation."[13]

Allen and other authors of this address believed that "to obviate these evils and with a desire of raising the moral and political standing of ourselves, we cannot devise any plan more likely to accomplish this end, than by encouraging agriculture and mechanical arts." The results of such a program would produce a phenomenon that we called viability in a previous chapter but is articulated by Allen as "a degree of independence, which as yet has fallen to the lot of but few of us." Furthermore, the "faithful pursuit" of agricultural and mechanical arts would "expand and ennoble the mind and would eventually give us the standing and condition we desire."

That Allen and others could believe that mechanical and agricultural arts could "ennoble the mind" would be met with some degree of incredulity and disdain by thinkers such as W. E. B. DuBois seventy years later. Yet on the other hand, their stance would not be entirely identified with the one taken by Booker T. Washington, DuBois's adversary, who argued that classical education and disciplines were essentially irrelevant to the preferred economic development of a black southern peasantry.

During the 1830s, Allen and others who were articulating the role of prudence in the development of African American integrity believed that the fruits of prudence, the ability to discern avenues for race uplift, did not fit into neat categories as the Washington–DuBois debate suggested. For them this debate would probably be a meaningless abstraction. Allen and the other signers of this address focused their attention primarily on the practical uses of education, but they still could see how even this type of education could "ennoble the mind."

Other commentators in this decade saw the clear value of a more practical bent to education. An editorial in the March 4, 1837, edition of the *Colored American* averred that to elevate the race, "Our sons must not be made classic drones, our daughters polished flirts. Let us rather teach our sons commerce, mechanism and agriculture, and make them the mechanics and producers of the land. As to our daughters, let us give them solid education, especially not neglect needlework and domestic economy."[14]

The link between education and elevation was further articulated at the Second Annual Convention of People of Colour when it was affirmed that "Education, Temperance and Economy are best calculated to promote the elevation of mankind to a proper rank and standing among men, as they enable him to discharge all those duties enjoined on him by his Creator."[15] The virtuous life could not be contemplated or adequately pursued, it was felt, except by appropriation and nourishment of the arts of the mind.

The power of enlightened intellect to bring about a measure of black uplift also was extended to produce significant changes in the society. The hope was that education could counter the forces of racism and oppression. James Forten Jr. believed that the process of elevating the people "from ignorance and superstition to light and knowledge" was

eminently calculated from its pure and holy designs to place us far beyond the reach of our ungenerous oppressors—to strip them of every chance by which they might assail us—to palsy the Herculean arm of prejudice—to change the scornful look, the invidious frown, into an approving smile—to force the rude laugh of contempt and ridicule into a silence deep and breathless as the eternal sleep of death.[16]

Behind this rather florid language is a basic assumption held by Forten and others on the matter of education: true and thorough education is the hallmark of civilized life; therefore civilized people pay it deference wherever it is encountered. "If we ever expect to see the influence of prejudice decrease," they believed, "it must be by the blessings of an enlightened education. It must be by being in possession of that classical knowledge which promotes genius, and causes man to soar up to those high intellectual enjoyments and acquirements, which places him in a situation to shed upon a country and a people, that scientific grandeur which is imperishable by time, and drowns in oblivion's cup their moral degradation."[17] Such was the hope of these black men and women who dared to believe that through virtue and the enlightened mind they could be accorded their due place within American civilization. Years later, Rev. J. W. C. Pennington would be able to write, "There is a deep conviction resting upon the minds of enlightened colored men throughout the world that the time has fully come for us to develop our attributes of manhood equally with the other races in the common work of Christian civilization."[18]

Young People's Education and Reading Societies

A second offshoot of this fascination with the world of ideas was a focus on the education of young people. In an oration of 1813, George Lawrence had articulated this link between cultivating an enlightened intellect among youth and the ability of such an intellect to counter oppression. In a celebration of the abolition of the U.S. slave trade, Lawrence implored his listeners in this way: "Let us cultivate the minds of youth; let your examples be clothed with wisdom and be strewed in their paths; by you let their tender minds be impressed with humane principles; let your virtues shine conspicuously before them, as lamps that shall light them to a glorious victory over their enemies."[19]

The call for colleges and normal schools issued at the 1832 Convention of Free People of Color was done precisely so that "our youth may be instructed in all the arts of civilized life." Austin

Steward admonished black people, "Let your attention be given to the careful training and education of the rising generation, that they may be useful and justly command the respect of their fellowmen."[20] When the Philadelphia Library Company for Colored Persons was organized on January 1, 1833, it noted in its incorporation papers: "We, the people of color of this city being deeply impressed with the necessity of promoting among our youth, a proper cultivation for literary pursuits and improvement of the faculties and powers of their minds."[21]

The convention minutes of 1831 took to task anyone who believed that only a rudimentary education would be adequate for black people, especially the young: "Those who think that our primary schools are capable of effecting this [sufficient education] are a century behind the age. . . . They [the primary schools] might have performed what was expected of them . . . but are now no longer capable of reflecting brilliance on our national character; which will elevate us from our present situation."[22] Rev. Amos Gerry Beman would be even more forceful in correlating education with the ability to repel oppression some thirty years later. In musing on the power of the enlightened mind, he could assert in 1859 that "more and more, the world is to be governed by the force of cultivated mind—superior intelligence will secure itself the 'lion's share of the spoil.'" Continuing in a paraphrase of Milton, Beman added, "To be ignorant is to be weak, and, to be weak is to be miserable."[23]

That a close link between education and the pursuit of virtue existed in the minds of many African Americans during this period is evident from the proliferation of clubs, societies, and sabbath schools dedicated to the cultivation of an enlightened intellect among black people. The African Clarkson Society became the first literary society for African Americans in New York City in 1829. Naming this society after Thomas Clarkson (1760–1846), the famous British abolitionist, suggests that in the minds of its founders a close connection was contemplated between mental acuity and the fight against slavery. An eponymous contributor to the *Colored American* named "Augustine" praised sabbath schools as not only "literary institutions where the arts and sciences were taught, but a [sic] moral one, in which youth received instruction in the duty to God, themselves, and society."[24]

In 1833, the Phoenix Society was formed to "promote the improvement of the colored people in morals, literature and the mechanic arts." Among its officers were significant black abolitionists such as Christopher Rush, Theodore S. Wright, Peter Williams, Charles B. Ray, and Samuel E. Cornish.[25] A year later the New York Garrison Literary Association, known also as the New York Garrison Literary and Benevolent Society, and the New York Female Literary Society were formed. Such clubs met a very practical need in the black community since blacks were not always welcome in public reading rooms. By 1837 the New York Philomathean Society made its approximately six hundred volumes available in order to satisfy the thirst for reading within the African American community.[26]

This intense desire among blacks to establish contexts in which the intellect could be honed and moral sensibility sharpened can be seen in the proliferation of literary clubs in other cities as well during the 1830s. The Philadelphia Association for Moral and Mental Improvement of the People of Color was organized in 1835; farther to the west in the same state, the Young Men's Literary and Moral Reform Society of Pittsburgh and Vicinity was formed in 1837. Well before 1835, a Mental and Moral Improvement Society had been formed among blacks in Troy, New York, while in Baltimore the Young Men's Mental Improvement Society for the Discussion of Moral and Philosophical Questions of All Kinds had been created.[27]

Of all the weapons African American proponents of virtue had at their disposal to fight injustice, they intuited that the virtue of prudence, wisdom, or critical discernment was foundational to all of the other cardinal virtues. Through prudence and the enlightened intellect a critical consciousness was possible, a consciousness by which they were able to speak forcefully against a social structure that sought to keep them in an inferior status. A critical consciousness also provided the means by which they would attack slavery and propose a vision of justice and the just state, the issue to which we now turn.

4

The Quest for Justice and the Just State

*We plead for the extension of those principles on which
our government was formed, that it in turn may become purified
from those iniquitous inconsistencies into which she has fallen
by her aberration from first principles.*

"Declaration of Sentiment,"

American Moral Reform Society, 1837

AFRICAN AMERICAN PROPONENTS of virtue affirmed a quest
for justice in U.S. society and the building of a virtuous state that
would be the radical alternative to the pernicious practice of state-
sanctioned slavery that was so averse to the practice and inculcation
of virtue. Such a state not only would be free of the scourge of slavery but also would be a society in which the rights, duties, and protection of every citizen would be guaranteed. But in what ways exactly did they conceive justice, and how was that vision articulated?

Fundamentally, there are two ways in which one might understand how justice is meted out or accomplished. One way is the *retributive* theory of justice. Understood primarily as a means of de-
vising appropriate punishment, this notion of justice seeks to give
back to malefactors the punishment they deserve. The classic example is the ancient "eye for an eye and tooth for a tooth" principle. The

other theory of justice is the *distributive* model, one that seeks to arrive at an equitable distribution of punishment and rewards on a just and fair basis. African American proponents of virtue would articulate both visions of justice as they sought to forge a place for themselves within the political structures of U.S. society.

Appeals for Retributive Justice

Given their universal hatred for the institution of slavery and their contempt for the U.S. government and its role in upholding that practice, it is not surprising that African American proponents of virtue tended to accentuate the retributive model of justice.

They were relentless in their denunciation of the moral outrage that constituted the practice of U.S. slavery. In his preamble to the *Appeal in Four Articles,* David Walker affirmed his inability to reconcile a view of God as a "God of justice" with that of a God who gave "peace and tranquility to tyrants, and permits them to keep our fathers, our mothers, ourselves and our children in eternal ignorance and wretchedness."[1]

For her part, Maria Stewart cast a fairly wide net in denouncing peoples and nations that had been tainted with the stain of slavery, Africa included. The "holy indignation" that filled the soul of Maria Stewart accounts in large measure for the stridency of her tone of denunciation of the American state and the segments of African states that had willingly participated in the slave trade.

She considered Africa's participation in the trade grievous, but consistent with the patterns of other ancient states that had experienced a rise and fall in political and economic fortunes. Africa's fall from grace was particularly tragic, since "we sprang from one of the most learned nations of the whole earth—from the seat, if not the parent of science; yes poor, despised Africa was once the resort of sages and legislators of other nations, was esteemed the school for learning, and the most illustrious men in Greece flocked thither for instruction."[2] Why did Africa fall? Her explanation was couched in terms redolent with theological assumptions and biblical imagery. "It was our gross sins and abominations that provoked the Almighty to frown thus heavily upon us, and give our glory unto others."

Africa thus joined other ancient peoples and powers that through intemperance and a lack of virtue succumbed to external aggressors after a period of internal moral decay. She viewed slavery as evidence of the wrath of God, for "he hath chasteneth you with the rod of his wrath, and hath deprived you of your kindred and friends; he hath sent death and pestilence among you, and many have become widows and their children fatherless; and still you go on unconcerned as though all were well, saying with proud Pharaoh, 'Who is the Lord, that we should obey him?'"[3]

But Stewart was equally, if not more, forceful in indicting the American nation for its role in enslaving the sons and daughters of Africa. This America she likened to the biblical whore of Babylon. Consistent with her sense of prophetic apocalypticism, she viewed the American nation as the great city that boasts in her heart, "I sit a queen, and am no widow, and shall see no sorrow" (Rev. 18:7 KJV). She went on to describe this American Babylon as a "seller of slaves and the souls of men; she has made Africans drunk with the wine of fornication; she has put them completely beneath her feet, and she means to keep them there; her right hand supports the reins of government; and her left hand the wheel of power, and she is determined not to let go her grasp."

Yet retribution and justice will come, believed Maria Stewart, for "many powerful sons and daughters of Africa will shortly arise." This retribution may be violent if need be, for these same sons and daughters of Africa will "declare by Him that sitteth upon the throne, that they will have their rights, and if refused, I am afraid they will spread horror and devastation around."

The "horror and devastation" of Maria Stewart's grim vision found replication in the thought of others. Austin Steward, who had been kidnapped and held a slave for twenty-two years, called for divine punishment of the United States. After recounting heartrending episodes of slave auctions and news of runaways who had been brutally murdered while attempting to escape slavery, Steward invoked the biblical wrath of God: "Shall I not visit for these things, saith the Lord; and shall not my soul be avenged on such a nation as this?"[4] On two notable occasions, the redoubtable Henry Highland Garnet prophesied a terrible rain of divinely ordered retributive justice upon the United States. In a eulogy to John Brown, that martyr in the cause for the abolition of slavery, Garnet told a New York City audience on the day of Brown's execution:

Often have I indulged the hope of seeing slavery abolished without the shedding of blood; but that hope is clouded. In the signs of the times, I see the dreadful truth, written as by the finger of Jehovah. For the sins of this nation there is no atonement without the shedding of blood. . . . The nation needed to see a picture of the future of slavery and its end and methinks God has been pleased to draw it in crimson.[5]

Six years later, as the nation was moving toward the concluding months of its great and bloody Civil War, Garnet could again indict the nation for its sins, this time as he spoke in the well of the U.S. Congress as a guest. Said Garnet in this Memorial Discourse:

Great sacrifices have been made by the people; yet greater still are demanded ere atonement can be made for our national sins. Eternal justice holds heavy mortgages against us; and will require the payment of the last farthing. We have involved ourselves in the sin of unrighteous gain, stimulated by luxury, and pride, and the love of power and oppression; and prosperity and peace can by purchased only by blood, and with tears of repentance. We have paid some of the fearful installments, but there are other heavy obligations to be met.[6]

Appeals for Distributive Justice

It is clear as well, however, that these African American proponents of virtue held out a vision of justice that took its inspiration from the distributive model. But they arrived at an articulation of this model through musings on the nature of the ideal state and the prospects of an American state that could incorporate them as full citizens. In such a state, a republic, could the virtue of justice finally be enjoyed.

These proponents of virtue drew the view of the ideal state from a classical political theory that vaunted the ideals of the republic. Such a state was made up of autonomous, free, self-ruling persons. Rev. H. Easton believed the genius of republican government rested in its contractual arrangements or "agreements of its subjects, relative to the disposal of their mutual interests." He also was of the opinion that "to the extent that these agreements were abrogated or the mutuality of interests frustrated by tyranny of any form, true republican government could not exist."[7] Moreover, Easton thought that virtue was absolutely necessary for good republican government. He held that "a republican form of government can be a blessing to no people, further than they make honest virtue the rule of life."

These proponents of virtue also drew upon the political theories that the founders of the Republic had used to undergird American Revolutionary consciousness—the idea of republican virtue and a government most consonant with that idea. The members of the American Moral Reform Society believed that "a pure, unmixed republicanism" was the form of government "best suited to the condition of men, by its promoting equality, virtue, and happiness to all within its jurisdiction."[8]

Republicanism had been the major political ideology to fuel the American revolt from England in the latter part of the eighteenth century. As a political system, republicanism attempted to hold power and liberty in a suitable degree of tension. Republican government was the interstice between the power wielded by rulers in the name of the people and the liberty the people themselves sought to exercise. Republican government affirmed that documents of law such as constitutions would provide adequate safeguards for both agents of power—rulers and the people in whose name the rulers wielded authority.

Such safeguards were necessary but not sufficient to ensure an equitable interplay between the aspirations of the people and the power of the rulers. Virtue, public and private, was the only element that could maintain this equilibrium between power and liberty. Maintenance of this equilibrium devolved in part upon the individuals of the republic, upon their willingness to exercise restraint and refrain from selfishness for the good of the whole. Expectedly, the proponents of virtue came to regard the state as a *moral* entity as well as a political entity. The legitimacy of the state rested on its ability to fulfill certain moral expectations.

William Hamilton, chairman of the Fourth Annual Negro Convention, told fifty delegates that the level of a state's moral fiber was directly related to its ability to be inclusive of all and not exclude people for purely arbitrary reasons. "Civilization is not perfect," said Hamilton, "until the community shall see that a wrong done to one is wrong done to the whole; that the interest of one is or ought to be the common interest of the whole. Surely that must be a happy state of society where the sympathies of all are to all alike."[9]

The institution of slavery, insofar as it was upheld by the U.S. government, belied the American pretensions at republican values. In noting the grave discrepancy between the republican ideals of the Revolutionary period and the present reality, Austin Steward cried out, "I would to God that America would arise in her native majesty and divest herself of the foul stain, which Slavery has cast upon her otherwise pure drapery."[10] Otis Ammidan and Isaac Barton authored an open letter to the people of the United States in 1825 that foreshadowed Lincoln's famous question posed on the fields of Gettysburg whether this nation "so conceived in liberty could long endure" half slave and half free. "We are trying," the two men asserted, "the great experiment, whether liberal Government is best calculated for the happiness of man; and its opposers seize with readiness the argument that one portion of our population is dependent for its luxuries, and even for its existence, on the abject servitude of another. The power of example is lessened, and patriotism turns with disgust from our practical application of that splendid theory, which declares that all men should be free and equal."[11]

Slavery, then, has not only robbed the slaves of their liberty but has also severely compromised the moral character and stature of the nation. William Wells Brown, who escaped from a particularly harsh life under slavery in 1821, lectured some twenty-six years later to the Female Anti-Slavery Society of Salem, Massachusetts, and articulated his views on this relationship between slavery and the moral and civic fabric of the nation: "The system of slavery . . . is a system that strikes at the foundation of society, that strikes at the foundation of civil and political institutions." It is, he continued, "a system that takes man down from that lofty position which his God designed that he should occupy; that drags him down, places him upon a level with the beasts of the field, and there keeps him, that it may rob him of his liberty."[12] In a letter to his former master, Capt. Enoch Price, Brown averred that "whatever in its proper tendency and general effect destroys, abridges, or renders insecure, human welfare, is opposed to the spirit and genius of Christianity." As for slavery itself, it is an institution that "sets at defiance the laws of God and the reason of man."[13]

Otis Ammidan and Isaac Barton, speaking for the Acting Committee of the American Convention for Promoting the Abolition of Slavery, considered slavery "to be contradictory to the laws of Nature

. . . in violation of the commandments of Christianity—hostile to our political union—inconsistent with our professed love of liberty—degrading to our national character."[14] William Wells Brown lamented, "It is deplorable to look at the character of the American people, the character that has been given to them by the institution of Slavery."[15] Persons who were directly involved in the institution learned to brutalize their slaves with impunity, a situation that for Brown could not help leading to a steady deadening of moral sensibility. Slavery also encouraged sexual license by permitting the concubinage of black women and the forced mating or separation of slave partners. Brown went on to discuss the incongruous situation in which churches, by receiving bequests from members' estates, could unwittingly become the owners of slaves and thus directly be involved in its great immorality. To the extent that some people profited directly from slavery and others indirectly, by consuming products or capital produced through slave labor, all of U.S. society was morally tainted by the institution.

This assessment forced him to declare that no distinction could be made between the people and their government insofar as culpability about slavery was concerned. Any distinction was purely artificial. "When I speak of the character of the American people," said Brown, "I look at the nation. I place all together, and draw no mark between the people and the government. Republicanism is dead long since, and yet we talk about democracy and republicanism, while one sixth of our countrymen are clanking their chains upon the very soil which our fathers maintained with their blood."[16]

Not only did the presence of slavery mar the integrity of the would-be republic, the imposition of political alienation on its free people of color constituted as well an affront to any pretense at being a republic. After being rebuffed by the Massachusetts Legislative Committee of the Militia for his attempts to form a black militia in 1853, William J. Watkins could say: "This is professedly a republican government; we are an integral portion of this Republic. We claim the absolute right, inalienable, God-given right as free men. . . . And no one has the right, *morally* speaking, either natural or acquired, to dehumanize and segregate us from the rest of mankind. You may withhold our right, but you cannot annihilate it."[17]

By constantly holding up the ideal of republicanism on which the United States was ostensibly based, they could point out the flaws in the existing political order. Numerous social institutions were singled out as evidence of the general paucity of true republicanism in U.S. society. Clearly, the political system and the state-sanctioned racism that protected slavery promoted doctrines at variance with the ideals of republican government.

Black theorists of the just political order demanded that the present political order seek to emulate the ideals of the initial aims of the republic. "We plead for an extension of those principles on which our government was formed," declared the American Moral Reform Society, "that it may in turn become purified from those iniquitous inconsistencies into which she has fallen by her aberration from first principles; that the laws of our country may cease to conflict with the spirit of that sacred instrument, the Declaration of Independence."[18] These thinkers came to view the Declaration and the other great document of the American state, the Constitution, as documents that had the power to indict Americans who treated a portion of the populace with a contempt unbefitting a true republic.

As if to grant near sacred status to these documents, and to ritually affirm them as such, the delegates to the First Annual Convention of Free Persons of Colour voted that both documents "be read in our conventions; believing that the truths contained in the former are incontrovertible, and that the latter guarantees in letter and spirit to every freeman born in this country, all the rights and immunities of citizenship."[19] When Henry Highland Garnet addressed the American Anti-Slavery Society during its seventh anniversary meeting in 1840, he asserted that "of the principles laid down in the Declaration of Independence, we find no fault." In Garnet's opinion, the fault lay in the "base conduct of [the] degenerate sons" of the authors of that document.[20]

Appeals to a Higher Justice and Its Laws

The concept of retributive justice helps explain why these African American proponents of virtue could indict the sham republic and foresee doom, destruction, and bloodletting if the country did not live up to its republican ideals. Yet the other vision of justice, distributive justice, played a role in their overall vision of the virtue of justice. The idea of distributive justice goes to the matter of relations between citizens and their relations with the government that wields power in their name. Distributive justice seeks to understand the basis for any mutuality that might exist between citizens themselves or between citizens and their government.

The Seeds of Critical Political Consciousness

It was patently clear to the African American proponents of virtue that as long as they were denied full and free access to the political and civil rights enjoyed by other Americans, the nation that perpetrated these wrongs would remain only a pale shadow of a true republic. As such then, the nation could not distribute to them justice in the fashion that a true republic could. But the hope was always there.

Frederick Douglass was able to fashion a view of distributive justice with the eventual reign of virtue and enlightenment. Said Douglass,

> The American government rests for support, more than any other government in the world, upon the loyalty and patriotism of all its people. The friendship and affection of her black sons and daughters, as they increase in virtue and knowledge, will be an element of strength to the Republic too obvious to be neglected and repelled. I predict, therefore, that under an enlightened public sentiment, the American people will cultivate the friendship, increase the usefulness and otherwise advance the interests of the colored race.[21]

It was evident that no substantial degree of distributive justice would be available within the U.S. political system until Douglass's prediction came true. But having acknowledged that, did African Americans feel obliged to obey the rules and laws of the nation, even though it was a flawed republic?

The record indicates some degree of ambiguity on this matter, some degree of respect for the notion of law, but a real aversion to the laws that oppressed them. There was a measure of double consciousness at work as the proponents of virtue sought to reconcile any contradictions in their fidelity to the laws of the republic while they repudiated its moral status.

A distinctive, conservative posture toward the state was expressed by many black thinkers of the 1830s, especially as reflected in the convention movement. In 1831 the address to the Second Annual

Convention for the Improvement of the Free People of Color admonished members: "Be righteous, be honest, be just, be economical, be prudent, offend not the laws of your country, in a word, live in that purity of life, by both precept and example."[22]

Such advice might seem incredibly tepid and unduly conciliatory to a system that oppressed them and a government that was a sham republic. But we might err if we believe that the proponents of virtue were seeking to comport themselves solely according to the laws of the United States. Their sights were much higher: fidelity to a sense of order and justice that stood higher than the confines of the inadequate republic.

As Thomas Hamilton, vigorous in the American Moral Reform movement of the 1830s and later editor of the *Anglo-African Magazine,* would put it, "Our cause is something higher, something holier than the founding of states. Our work is to purify the State."[23] And by obeying just laws, they would become exemplars of distributive justice everywhere. In the estimation of the members of the Second Annual Convention for the Improvement of the Free People of Color, adherence to the laws of the country would "render you illustrious in the eyes of civilized nations, when they will assert, that all that illustrious worth, which was once possessed by the Egyptians, and slept for ages, has now arisen in their descendants, the inhabitants of the new world."[24] In 1830 the Conventional Address had urged a similar admonition, couching it in the hope of acquiring "standing among the nations of the earth, as men and freemen."[25] The Conventional Address of 1830 admonished African Americans, "Endeavor to walk in circumspection: be obedient to the laws of our common country; honour and respect its lawmakers and lawgivers: and through it all, let us not forget to *respect ourselves.*"[26] Thus, U.S. laws should be obeyed in the spirit and intent of distributive justice. Theoretically, a distribution of justice closely followed the extent to which laws were obeyed.

The same proponents of virtue also expressed a belief that obeying the laws of even an imperfect state such as the United States could serve a nobler and higher cause. The Conventional Address of 1830 really suggested that even if respect from the U.S. system was not forthcoming, then at least self-respect could be gleaned as well as the knowledge that their behavior conformed with a higher standard of duty. Visions that went beyond the U.S. context were tied to visions including membership in the worldwide family of peoples in a "standing among the nations of the earth, as men and freemen," a commitment to the body of virtuous republicanism that stood as a stern measure indicting the utter poverty of the U.S. political system.

Being true to this universal vision was consistent with their fidelity to the God whom they considered ultimate and sovereign and the supreme Giver of law. An eloquent example is provided in the proceedings of the Fourth Annual Convention of Free People of Color, held in 1834. The Declaration of Sentiment sought to temper the naive exuberance inherent in some members' rush to embrace U.S. citizenship uncritically. The Declaration reminded them that U.S. law, even to the extent that it provided some semblance of protection from civic disorder, was used to uphold unrighteous slaveholding and was ultimately under a higher law—that of God. "Therefore, under whatever pretext or authority laws have been promulgated or executed, whether under parliamentary, colonial, or American legislation, we declare them in the sight of Heaven wholly null and void, and should be immediately abrogated."[27]

If it entails support of unjust laws, citizenship is to be spurned from this perspective: "Let us not lament, that under the present constituted powers of this government, we are disfranchised; better far than to be partakers of its guilt. Let us refuse to be allured by the glittering endowments of official station or enchanted with the robe of American citizenship. But let us choose like true patriots, rather to be the victims of oppression, than the administrators of injustice."

Appealing to the ultimate sovereignty of God, under whom stands the U.S. system in all of its pale imitation of true virtuous republicanism, the signers of the Declaration stated their position as "patriots" in this moving statement:

> Therefore our only trust is in the agency of divine truth, and the spirit of American liberty; our cause is glorious and must finally triumph. Though the blighting hand of time, should sweep us from the stage of action; though other generations should pass away, our principles will live forever; we will teach our children, and our children's children, to hand them down to unborn generations, and to the latest posterity; not merely for the release of the bondman from his chains, nor for the elevation of the free coloured

man to the privileges of citizenship; nor for the restoration of the world from infidelity and superstition, but from the more fatal doctrine of expediency, without which the true principles of religion can never be established, liberty never secure, or the sacred rights of man remain inviolate.[28]

The sovereignty of God ultimately provided for those patriots of the ideal and true republic the proper context in which to judge the flawed U.S. political system.

And such a sovereign God not only judges the politically unjust but also succors the politically oppressed. "He hates all oppression, resists the proud tyrant," thundered Rev. J. W. C. Pennington, a runaway blacksmith slave who later forged a career as an abolitionist minister, "[and] He loves the poor and has promised deliverance to the captive."[29] Even Frederick Douglass, who it is to be suspected always kept a skeptic's distance from religious fervor, could write in commenting on the human limitations in the quest for abolition: "We shall therefore, continue to look to the God of the oppressed, who can see the end from the beginning, for strength and guidance in whatever the future may have in store for us."[30]

Thus, when the free black proponents of virtue of the 1830s and thereafter admonished their brothers and sisters to obey the laws of the state, the admonition was not given out of a sense of slavish sycophancy toward the state. Far from it. Laws of the United States should be obeyed unless obedience would further the aims of tyranny. And besides that, there was the belief that when weighed in the great balance of scales of virtuous republicanism countenanced by a sovereign God, the entire U.S. system stood, relatively speaking, on a rather insignificant level. Samuel H. Davis, chairman of the 1843 National Convention of Colored Citizens, pointedly said, "We love our country, we love our fellow-citizens—but we love liberty more."[31]

The love of liberty for African American proponents of virtue was grounded in an absolute belief in a just moral universe, superintended by a just God. A way was available to understand the deep structures underlying this just moral universe, and that way was the cultivation and enlightenment of the mind, or the acquisition of the virtue of prudence. So armed, the people in their struggle for freedom and justice could proceed apace with vigor and courage. It is to the virtue of courage, or fortitude, that we now turn.

5

The Virtue of Fortitude—
"Keepin' On a-Keepin' On"

It is perseverance we want; let us get hold of this.

James Forten Jr.

Address to the American Moral Reform Society,

August 17, 1837

AFRICAN AMERICAN PROPONENTS of virtuous life, a life in
which the enlightened intellect would be impelled to struggle for justice, affirmed the cardinal virtue of fortitude. In terms of order, fortitude has been considered the third among the cardinal virtues. Its dependence upon prudence and justice affords it a rationale and vision
for sustained and arduous engagement in life. As Josef Pieper aptly
put it: "Without prudence, without justice, there is no fortitude; only
he who is just and prudent can also be brave; to be really brave is quite
impossible without at the same time being prudent and just also."[1]

African American proponents of virtue envisioned a U.S. political system that would accord them justice and a society in which
they could interact with other citizens in a just fashion. The ability
to sustain a campaign against injustice and oppression required fortitude. Having been denied a place within the social structures of a
society purely on the arbitrary basis of race, the African American
exponents of virtue affirmed a place for themselves in an ordered
moral universe that was beyond the parochial bounds of American
racist society. The depth of such affirmation required a level of forti-

64

tude in their struggle against racism and the institution of slavery. Their vision of virtue afforded them a measure of fortitude without which their struggle might have foundered.

A Moral Universe and Cultivated Minds

Fortitude, it seems, drew its strength and inspiration from at least two sources for these proponents of virtue. First, they were able to draw sustained strength for the struggle through the belief in a moral universe that appeared to support their cause against slavery and oppression. There was a great moral struggle between good and evil, virtue and vice, freedom and slavery, and they were squarely in the thick of it.

William Watkins saw those forces arrayed against each other quite clearly in a speech he gave to the Moral Reform Society of Philadelphia. To an audience of other black people engaged in the struggle against oppression, he stated, "On the one hand we see arrayed against us an unblushing piety, unholy pride, groveling sinful prejudice, and a shortsighted worldly policy." But juxtaposed to those forces was "an invincible phalanx of all that is liberal and magnanimous, holy, just and good—the active sympathies of the civilized world, and the moral energies of the universe." Watkins ended his oration by declaring confidently, "Ours is a righteous cause—that of our enemies, an unrighteous one."[2]

James Forten Jr. (the son of the wealthy Philadelphia sail maker James Forten Sr., who led protest efforts among northern blacks in the early nineteenth century) encouraged the women, black and white, of the Ladies' Anti-Slavery Society of Philadelphia by tapping into this reservoir of divine presence in the moral universe. Said young Forten to them: "You are called fanatics. Well, what if you are? Ought you to shrink from this name? God forbid. There is an eloquence in such fanaticism, for it whispers hope to the slave; there is a sanctity in it, for it contains the consecrated spirit of religion."[3]

In his celebration of the end of slavery in New York in 1827, Rev. Nathaniel Paul surely moved his audience by sharing with them his vision of a changed world when at long last, slavery would have been abolished everywhere. "How changed shall then be the aspect of the moral and political world!" he exulted. "Africa, elevated to more than her original dignity, and redressed for the many aggravated and complicated wrongs she has sustained, with her emancipated sons, shall take her place among the other nations of the earth. The iron manacles of slavery shall give place to the still stronger bonds of brotherly love and affection, and justice and equity shall be the governing principles that shall regulate the conduct of men of every nation." But for that day to come, a requisite level of courage and hope would have to be summoned forth. Paul concluded his message with a desire to see this level of courage attained: "Influenced by such motives, encouraged by such prospects, let us enter the field with a fixed determination to live and to die in the holy cause."[4]

That Watkins, Forten, and others could speak with such confidence was due also to a profound belief that a divine presence was ultimately superintending the moral universe. The perception of God's will and intent, even in the midst of African American suffering, accounts for a discernible measure of hope within the dark apocalyptic vision of Maria Stewart. Stewart had joined her vision of moral purity with an apocalyptic vision of political and social upheaval that would eventuate in a radically changed moral and social order. Hers was a theological vision, heavily indebted to the prophetic consciousness of the Hebrew Scriptures and notions of a wrathful God.

Yet precisely because Stewart's vision was so cast in theological terms, there was a provision for atonement and ultimate redemption through the graciousness of God. While "sin and prodigality have caused the downfall of nations, kings and emperors (Africa's included), were it not that God in wrath remembers mercy, we might indeed despair." She rejoiced in the fact that Divine Providence had secured the destiny of the race with the promise that "Ethiopia shall again stretch forth her hands unto God."[5] God would surely act to redeem God's people in the future, to the extent that they espoused a renewed sense of virtue.

Second, they were able to draw strength for fortitude from the belief that the enlightened and cultivated mind could alter circumstances and the realities around them. In the hostile society in which they lived, they believed, perhaps with a naiveté that comes with single-mindedness, that the benefits of the enlightened mind would have definite social effects.

Delegates to the Second Annual Convention of Free People of Color in 1831, for example, affirmed,

If we ever expect to see the influence of prejudice decrease, and ourselves respected, it must be by the blessings of an enlightened education. It must be by being in possession of that classical knowledge which promotes genius and carries man to soar to those high intellectual enjoyments which place him in a situation to shed upon a country and a people that scientific grandeur which is imperishable by time.[6]

Clearly, the delegates who agreed to this statement hoped that classical education and an enlightened mind would counter and dissipate the oppressive forces around them.

The imagery within such a process was described in a fascinating way by Robert Gordon, a rather obscure black intellectual at midcentury who published an article entitled "Intellectual Culture" in the June 1859 issue of the *Anglo-African Magazine.*

Gordon attempted to conceive of the struggle of the mind against a seemingly unyielding environment in very active and dynamic terms. Such a struggle constituted in good measure an intellectual effort that could shape events and circumstances, rather than merely being a passive part of a context shaped by events and circumstances. Gordon began his thesis by asserting that in any well-regulated and balanced society, moral sensitivity and intellectual rigor were of equal importance; there must be a balance between heart and head. He viewed the Reign of Terror following the French Revolution as an example of a society set morally adrift, trusting too much in the pursuits of pure intellect. The rabid anticlericalism of that period was an example for him of "atheistical and diabolical conspiracy against Jehovah's August throne."[7] At the same time, Gordon perceived the danger of a society governed only by sentiment and custom. With the "cultivated faculties not being present to diffuse their enlightened rays on men and things under their influence, the atmosphere of that society cannot but partake of Gothic rarefaction," or be without real substance.

The dialectic between the two thrusts—the moral and the intellectual—takes place within Gordon's very specialized conception of the eventual role of education in society. For him education links enlightenment and purposeful action into an act very much similar to what sociologists of knowledge term "world building."[8] The truly educated mind is able to arrange the variables in one's environment so that a *moral* world appears; such a mind begins to prepare harbingers of change in the world, for a new world appears whenever one is transformed by education. So transformed persons with enlightened intellect are able to change their world around them.

Gordon explained his point of view by asking his reader to imagine

> an unshapely, ugly, hard substance against which my foot strikes, and causes me pain—what is it—why, a stone that I am very much disposed to hurl away in impotent anger for being the offensive object of my pain; but on a minute inspection, I am led to conclude that it would amply repay my industry were I to educate it. And now commences the mode of operation; the incrustations and the enveloping laminae are peeled off, and my eyes are gladdened by the sight of its intrinsic virtue; cleaning it, its natural beauty appears. By education, then, I become the possessor of a magnificent, beautiful gem.[9]

Behind this rather obscure bent of Gordon's language lies a disarmingly original conception of the role of education in society, which involves two important functions: critiquing or deconstructing the world and *remaking* or reconstructing the world.

Gordon understood the subversive *and* creative possibilities of genuine education. One might discern in his theory the assertion that while social structures *appear* to have a characteristic of permanence about them, they are in fact quite malleable. The critical consciousness that education fosters allows a person to discern the "incrustations and the enveloping laminae" of society. Such a consciousness enables a person to fully understand the underlying relations between human beings and their social world. This view was reflected by another thinker of the period, M. H. Freeman, who held that "a perfect education implies a clear and just *perception* of the varied relations man sustains to his Maker, to his fellow men and to himself."[10] For Gordon, a "magnificent, beautiful gem" comes to be as a result of exertion subsequent to the application of critical consciousness. Social structures, especially structures like slavery that had been upheld by ignorance, fear, and custom, could thus be shattered.

Gordon believed that education could undermine oppressive structures, and thus, one sees how he understood education in a uniquely active fashion. Education as world building meant that it and enlightenment would have to go far beyond the selfish enterprise of one person gaining knowledge for the sake of oneself. Indeed, it was as if the destiny of the race was involved when contemplating the role of education in African American society.

Bravery and Perseverance

The level of fortitude of a moral and just universe and the ability of the enlightened human mind to change circumstances in society account in part for the bravery and the ability to risk persecution in defiance against unjust laws. Even during the 1830s, when virtually all abolitionists, black and white, were moral suasionists—that is, those believing that only individual regenerated hearts would be the surest foundation for ending slavery—the African American members of the American Moral Reform Society were not reluctant to engage in political action to reach that goal.

A resolution that was passed at the 1835 convention of the American Moral Reform Society, at which moral suasionists were in the majority, attests to this: "Resolved that our duty to God, and to the principles of human rights, so far exceeds our allegiance to these laws that return the slave again to the master, (from the free states), that we recommend our people to peaceably bear the punishment those inflict rather than aid in returning their brethren to slavery."[11]

We can discern, therefore, within the thinking of these African American proponents of virtue an exaltation of the virtue of fortitude, the ability to persevere in the midst of daunting circumstances, and even the ability to alter such circumstances through the power of the enlightened mind. In assessing the entire record of their thought, we need to remember this dynamic aspect of the virtue of fortitude. That was necessary lest fortitude devolve into a merely reactionary and passive virtue.

A good example of a black mind wrestling with this problem inherent in a consideration of the virtue of fortitude is seen in an anonymously authored article that appeared in the September 1859 issue of the *Anglo-African Magazine*. Apparently, the impetus for writing the article was the writer's desire to refute a public remark about the natural inferiority of persons of color. The writer took umbrage at such a remark, but focused the article response in such a way that it became a vehicle for speculation into the nature of how races or cultural groups progress.

The author made a distinction between the power to endure effects and the power to effect consequences. Two terms were introduced—*vis inertia* and *vis insita*—to correspond respectively to these two types of power. The writer speculated that perhaps in matters of sheer survival, the power to endure, or *vis inertia*, blacks may be superior to whites. Yet this trait is not necessarily a particularly noteworthy one: "We hold it in common with the feline race. It is a species of standstillism—tough, wiry, malleable—very different from that *vis insita*, which is, as it were, a steam engine within a man, a race."

For this writer the more noteworthy power is the power to do, to be able to effect a change in circumstance. Even as this author indulged to some degree in questionable racism, as in the reference to a "feline race," and the image of the "steam engine within a . . . race," an aim in the article was to rebuff popular stereotypical notions about black people.

Some blacks and some sympathetic but paternalistic whites held the stereotype that although blacks do not equal whites in pursuit of material gain or mastery of technology, they may equal or surpass them "in another direction—that of love." The writer of "A Word to Our People," however, was not persuaded that love was as marked a phenomenon within the black community or even of the advisability of its being the predominant trait of a race, especially to the exclusion of more material pursuits.[12]

He believed the attributed love principle was vastly overrated within the African American community. "We do not love one another," he lamented; "we do not coalesce, agglutinate, organize on this principle, nor on any other."[13] Even the benevolent and mutual aid societies "and others of pious nomenclature of which we have more than our proportion are not love in their manifestation." He viewed them essentially and perhaps a bit too critically as manifesting an ideal "no higher than instinct of preservation against the force of circumstances which tend to crush us." They belong to *vis inertia* rather than to *vis insita*.

But even if it was granted that somehow love was the predominant trait of the race, the writer would have been skeptical of its presumed consequences, especially in comparison with the motivating force underlying more materialist pursuits. "If love be our predominant characteristic, have we manifested it in a degree analogous to that power which cuts through rocks a pathway for the locomotive—which beats, with foot-falls, a pathway across the "Isthmus of Chagres—which peoples Oregon and Wisconsin? We think not."[14]

Apparently, in reciting these accomplishments the writer was thinking of other races, whites perhaps in particular, who had accomplished them. Conversely, the writer chided blacks to the extent that they had not manifested the energy to perform such feats or feats commensurate at least with the presumed power of the love principle. Such deficiency is to be explained, the author surmised, "because we have a lower *ideal* than the whites. We aim less high, and therefore, require and use less force, in attaining our aim."

Yet from all of the tone of criticism did not come any suggestion that whites be mimicked or fawningly emulated: "We must, with all our oppression and degradation pressing upon us, look up, above, *beyond the whites* and determine to whip, to beat, to excel them. Let us at once cease all other work and stamp this impress on our souls. We must excel our oppressors." Such excelling would in all probability include acquiring proficiency in material pursuits such as commerce and the economic life, for "these are things which will come part and parcel of every honest effort to advance." Yet the author of "A Word to Our People" soberly advised that "in selecting our ideal, let us look . . . to the state of society in advance of the present, or wealth worshiping society."

If an object of emulation was ever to be found, it was not necessarily to be found within the culture of other races or within the mere accumulation of wealth. It was to be an ideal that transcended the particular accomplishment of races, specifically whites. In this regard Austin Steward had also earlier admonished his readers to "cease looking to the white man for example and imitation." Steward, as well as Douglass, refused to allow virtues such as industry and advancement to be the sole preserve of whites. He urged blacks to stand "boldly up in your own national characteristics, and show that by your perseverance and industry, your honor and purity, that you are men, colored men, but of no inferior quality."[15]

The perseverance of which Austin Steward spoke, or the virtue of fortitude as articulated by other African American proponents of virtue, factored in the continuing struggle for justice and the fight against oppression. Grounded firmly within the belief in a just and moral universe, the structures of which could be discerned by an enlightened intellect, they were thus able to secure a necessary measure of fortitude for that struggle.

Perhaps no more eloquent testimony to the power of this virtue of fortitude and endurance within the African American spirit can be found than in the words of Rev. J. W. C. Pennington. On the eve of the great national conflict that would end slavery, Pennington could extol the relationship between hope and endurance:

> The past history of the descendants of Africa is now appealing to her sons and daughters in the four quarters of the globe, to be up and doing for God, for Christ, for the race, for pure religion, for humanity, for civilization, and for righteousness and truth. The response is certainly very creditable to the hoping and hopeful man: for such is the colored man the world over; for if their [*sic*] is a human being on the face of the earth who can hope alone, and even hope against hope, it is the colored man. And this is the secret of his amazing powers of endurance.[16]

African American proponents of virtue could avail themselves of the hope that could shore up the virtue of courage in the midst of their struggle against injustice and oppression. It is surely doubtful that without such endurance and fortitude, grounded in a hope in God's justice and their ability to prudently discern the political exertions that such justice demanded, the successful completion of their struggle could have come to pass.

6

TEMPERANCE AND THE
QUEST FOR CHARACTER

Let us use every exertion in our power
to promote the principles of temperance; as, by so doing,
we will greatly aid the cause of Education, Temperance,
Economy and Universal Love.

John Francis Cook

Address to the American Moral Reform Society,

August 16, 1837

CONTEMPORARY AND POPULAR NOTIONS of "temperance" are generally at odds with the meaning of the term as understood in its classical sense. People today are inclined to understand temperance as a valued desire to reduce excess, to achieve moderation in, say, eating and drinking. Josef Pieper is helpful again in suggesting that *temperantia* reveals a much wider range of significance than merely avoiding excess. The original meaning of the word has to do with "the virtue which realizes the inner order" within human beings.[1] Temperance seeks to bring ordered unity to all of the disparate and sometimes conflictual yearnings within us.

Temperance, then, lies not in restraint from doing too much of anything, but in a general sobriety of living in which a person controls what can be controlled and does not attempt to control what cannot be controlled.[2] Indeed, the word "self-control" has come to be synonymous with "temperance." However, the aim of self-control

is not so much to steer a middle path between extremes; rather, the
real object of self-control, and that of temperance, is to be able to
choose activities and commitments in life well within one's ability to
fulfill them.

The intemperate person is without such an ability to choose
rightly (thus indicating the close link with prudence, a prior cardinal
virtue); such inability is often the reason for moral and physical dissipation. Such a life has no order because there is absent a principle of
choosing rightly, or ordering options to be acted upon or pursued.
Temperance, therefore, connotes an ability to choose and, by so doing,
establish a valued order within spheres of living. In a very real sense,
temperance betokens a measure of power over one's surroundings.

African American proponents of virtue exhorted one another to
embody the virtue of temperance inasmuch as they believed that an ordered life would ultimately be the surest counterweight against social
forces that either demeaned or threatened the viability of African American existence. American racism always sought ways, in their judgment,
to undermine and instill aspects of chaos, or precariousness, within
African American life. The virtue of temperance signaled the importance of establishing an inner core of the self, a means by which African
Americans could affirm self-identity as free, self-regulating, and autonomous beings. The virtue of temperance and the concept of character help us understand how this measure of self-identity was articulated.

Character and Value

In an attempt to understand the process by which persons develop as
moral beings, the concept of character has proved immensely helpful
and fruitful. Interestingly enough, the *Oxford English Dictionary* de-
rives the word "character" from the Greek for an "instrument for
marking and graving, impress, stamp, distinctive mark, distinctive
nature." A person's character, following this literal meaning, might be
understood to be the habits and dispositions that appear to be indelibly "etched" within the personality. Indeed, one's character can be
formed according to upbringing, training, circumstances—all the
forces that shape human lives. As such, then, we cannot avoid at some
level associating character with one's identity, how a person is known.

As an ethical reality, character also involves the issue of value.
Presumably, we desire to be known in ways that correspond with

traits and characteristics we value. Character, all that has gone into shaping our identities, must at some point have a value dimension attached to it. African American proponents of virtue understood and articulated character as the set of valued habits and dispositions that would ensure a desired level of racial uplift and integrity and by which they could be identified.

The suggestion has been made throughout this book that all of the cardinal virtues are in some fashion related to one another and mutually reinforcing. African American proponents of virtue saw clearly the relationship between prudence, or the enlightened intellect, and temperance.

William Watkins was another energetic lecturer who affirmed the role of education in forming the virtuous life. Education cultivated the whole person and became thus an "inexhaustible source of refined pleasure," prompting a person to pursue intellectual enjoyments in the "lecture halls, the moral lyceum or the hall of science, rather than pursuing the more venal enticements in gambling and houses of vice."[3]

Many, such as James Forten Jr., the namesake of the famed and courageous northern black leader, spoke of the metamorphic power of education in the process of character development. Said young Forten,

> Education molds the character; it is the food of morality, nourishing the mental faculties, checking the tide of vice, subduing the violent passions and natural depravity which pervade the human breast; it renders man an ornament to society, a beautiful, intellectual and virtuous being; it gives him to know fully his relation to the Deity, inspires him with a dignity, possesses him with a commending mien, of which no power on earth can disrobe him.[4]

A vision of temperance was indissolubly linked with a vision of a just moral universe, a context in which all virtuous strivings would find vindication. Rev. Joseph Corr, in his address to the Humane Mechanics Society, averred that "Virtue, howsoever discouraged or oppressed for awhile shall not be deprived of that eternal reward which an impartial and unchangeable God has promised to all who are obedient to the mandates of heaven, without distinctions or exceptions of nations or colours."[5] Corr was not naive, however, in his estimations of the extent of evil and inequities in society. He saw a distinction between the natural order of things and the social, or moral, order that human beings create and maintain. While, in his words, "in the natural world nothing is redundant, nothing deficient, it is in the moral world only that we discover irregularity and defect. It falls short of that order and perfection which appears in the rest of creation." For Corr, "apparent disorder and social inequities are but reflections of the imperfect status of the moral world."

How are such "disorders" to be rectified? Corr assumed that certain powers were at work in the world that would lead to an eventual harmony in the moral world, a harmony that already existed in the natural world. The powers were manifested, first, in the "government of a Supreme Being, so full of truth and love as the great Governor of the universe," and second, in the purposive human will toward moral uprightness.

There is movement, then, in Corr's view of the way virtue can have consequences in the real world. He believed that a "just and equitable state of things shall be the success and crowning triumph of virtue, and the laurel wreath of victory shall distinguish all its persevering votaries." Human beings, insofar as they live the virtuous life, are "persevering votaries" of virtue; they produce actions and ultimately a state of society that is in harmony with the "great Governor of the universe."[6] A life of virtue, of tempered disposition, best ensured that a human being could become one of the "persevering votaries" so needed in the imperfect and flawed moral order of human societies.

The most obvious example of an imperfect and flawed moral order was the one in which they lived and which plagued them as persons of color. As African Americans surveyed the cultural landscape of the early nineteenth century, virtually all of the images of them held by their oppressors were demeaning and derogatory. Just as there was no room for blacks within the political process, there was no place for them among the respected and accepted members of "polite society," literally those welcomed into the affairs of the polis, those having a legitimate place among citizens. Blacks were thus identified as the unwelcome "other."

Consequently, the idea of virtue provided black thinkers with the basic material with which to forge an identity that could counter the obviously false and racist notions held by their oppressors. Racist ideology sought to erode and vitiate any notion of black persons as having any strength of character or integrity. There would thus emerge during this period a passion among African Americans for the building of "character," a means of self- and racial identification that would be a counterfoil to racist views of a deficient black personality and identity.

Character, for them, grew best in the soil of temperance. In his address to the members of the Humane Mechanics Society, Corr sought to dispel any notion that the practice of virtue consigned a person to a life of tedium and self-abnegation. He was of the opinion that "though virtue, at first sight, may appear to contract the bounds of enjoyment, it will be found upon a persevering practice, that in truth it enhances it." Corr went on to say, "If it restrains the excess of some pleasures, it enlarges and increases others; it precludes from none but such as are either fantastic and imaginary, or pernicious and destructive: whatever is truly valuable in human enjoyment it allows to a good man. . . . It not only allows him such pleasures, but heightens them, by that grateful relish which a good conscience gives to every pleasure."[7]

Although virtue and character were appreciated for their inherent value, African American proponents of virtue thought that character building could play a decisive role in quite practical terms, the most pressing being the aim of securing an acceptable level of "elevation" or "uplift" for the race. A clear correlation was made between social activism, moral reform, and race uplift in the minds of these thinkers. Indeed, as Leonard Sweet has observed, "There seems not to have been a single black abolitionist who did not merge his crusade to end slavery and prejudice with the contemporary crusade for moral reform and self-improvement. Indeed, emancipation and elevation were often seen as opposite sides of the same coin."[8]

The editorial in the first edition of the *Colored American—The Weekly Advocate* newspaper, published on January 7, 1837, gives us some indication of the underlying aims and dynamics of this process. The paper, printed and published by Robert Sears, had as its masthead "Established for and Devoted to the Moral, Mental, and Political Improvement of the People of Color." The editorial suggested that the paper would fill a vacuum: "It will be devoted to the moral improvement and amelioration of our race." The paper would also be an agent for unity: "The Advocate will be like a chain, binding you together as ONE." The editorial concluded by urging its readers to "rouse up and exert all their power, encouraged, and sustaining this effort which we have made to disabuse the public mind of the misrepresentations made of our character; and to show to the world, that there is virtue among us, though concealed; talent, though buried; intelligence, though overlooked."[9]

Race Elevation and Racial Unity

Elevation meant certain practical achievements: economic integrity, more literacy and educational advancement, and a greater sense of the race's worth in the surrounding society. In short, the quest for elevation was the quest for existential viability in a society that sought to impose contingency upon blacks. Elevation proffered the hope that the race could bestir itself to material and cultural ascendancy through the vigorous employment of spiritual and ethical values.

Intemperate habits were judged to be harmful to the prospect of the race achieving a desired level of elevation. William Watkins and others were concerned that such immoral pursuits not dissipate the energies of the race, for all of its vigor would be needed to do battle against the dreaded enemy of white racism.

Maria Stewart admonished the free blacks who had managed to acquire some economic resources and who had developed wasteful habits to "flee from the gambling board and the dance hall, for we are poor and have no money to throw away. Let our money, instead of being thrown away as heretofore, be appropriated for schools and seminaries of learning for our children and youth."[10] Against what she perceived to be rampant materialism infecting the morals of the black community, she railed, "Turn, O ye sons of Africa, turn your mind from these perishable objects, and content for the cause of God and the rights of man."

Implicit in Maria Stewart's prophetic stance was a call to moral purity that had social implications. She viewed those among the race who were self-indulgent, who were more interested in "perishable objects," and those whose lifestyle was improvident as directly opposed to those who were engaged in the "cause of God" and righteousness. For Stewart, righteousness had a social consequence in the real world of oppressed people; its ideal was realized in the crucible of oppression. Whatever dissipated their moral strength or sapped their economic integrity was unrighteous. The righteous were those who contended for the cause of God and for the rights of human beings, and who followed her admonition to support schools, seminaries, and other institutions of human nurturing. The righteous "shall shine in the kingdom of heaven as the stars forever and ever; while the slothful and negligent shall be bound hand and feet, and cast into outer darkness."[11]

While Stewart held out the vision of violent retribution at the hands of the sons and daughters of Africa, she envisioned a moral regeneration among them as well. They would "put down vice and immorality among us." Moreover, their moral zeal would inspire one another to cease to drink the "wine of Babylon's fornication." For Stewart, the acquisition of virtue and the shedding of vice would produce a sufficient degree of spiritual energy within the race that would enable it to expiate its own historic sin and allow it to repel the ravages imposed upon it by the American Babylon. She said, "I am of the strong opinion that the day on which we unite, heart and soul, and turn our attention to knowledge and improvement, that day the hissing and reproach among the nations of the earth against us will cease. And even those who now point at us with the finger of scorn will aid and befriend us."[12]

Crucial also to the regeneration and her vision of racial redemption and uplift was her conception of the role that virtue could play as a rallying point for establishing racial unity and integrity. According to her, acts that destroy the social bond between oppressed blacks should be denounced as ethically irresponsible acts, such acts wherein "our fathers have dealt treacherously with another, and because many of us now possess that envious and malicious disposition that we had rather die than see each other rise an inch above a beggar."[13] She believed that "never will the chains of slavery and ignorance burst, till we become as one, and cultivate amongst ourselves the pure principles of piety, morality and virtue."

Thus, Maria Stewart preached to the black community the notion that the pursuit of virtue could become the central motif of African American life, the realization of which could repel the aims of racist society, the work of the American Babylon, and also bring a degree of integrity and wholeness within the black community. Virtue for her was purposive and instrumental, and yet it signaled genuine moral regeneration within each person who pursued it and sought to live according to its demands. Her message sought to muster the energies of the oppressed and dispirited members of the black community, many of whom, in her opinion, were allowing the guile of the American Babylon to prevent them from reaching their rightful destiny of "stretching forth their hands unto God."

Achieving such ascendancy meant therefore undergirding the pragmatic concerns of elevation with an intangible world of enduring values. Even liberation from slavery would ultimately require of freed persons a measure of inner character so that the state of freedom might be sustained.

In an address celebrating the ending of slavery in New York State, Rev. Nathaniel Paul, pastor of the First African Baptist Society of Albany, addressed those concerns. In thundering oratory, he denounced the institution of slavery in striking terms, affirming "that our God is a God of justice, and no respecter of persons."[14] Paul hoped that the day would come when "men will be respected according to their character, and not according to their complexion, and when vices alone will render them contemptible."

Having thus established virtue and character as the true and essential indicators of human worth rather than material or social circumstances, Paul could then go on to suggest that character always superseded circumstance. "What," he asked, "is liberty without virtue?" In Paul's sober estimation, "it tends to lasciviousness, and freedom to the profligate is but a curse." Paul ended his celebratory message, anticipating forthrightly the joys and responsibilities of freedom:

> Brethren, we have been called into liberty: only let us use that liberty as not abusing it. This day commences a new era in our history; new scenes, new prospects, open before us, and it follows as a necessary consequence, that new duties devolve upon us; duties, which if properly attended to, cannot fail to improve our moral condition, and elevate us to a rank of respectable standing with the community; or if neglected, we fall at once into the abyss of contemptible wretchedness.[15]

Even for as pragmatic a man as Frederick Douglass, without such intangibles as a true sense of virtue, the process of elevation would be aborted. Douglass believed that the granting of full political and social privileges as U.S. citizens and economic security—the realities associated with elevation—would be to no avail if the race had not acquired a sense of character beforehand. "A change in our political condition," thought Douglass, "would do very little for us without this."[16] Character, for Douglass, was the constellation of virtues without which legitimate participation in the body politic would be unthinkable. He had in mind such virtues as "industry, sobriety, honesty, combined with intelligence, and a due self-respect."

In Douglass's estimation, the possession of such virtues would have a distinctly functional role in preserving the existential viability of the race. But Douglass did not view these virtues as race specific, or the sole possession of any race. Their legitimacy did not inhere in their being exemplified only by white people. These virtues, in and of themselves, were the rightful things that commanded respect, not the color of the person. "Find them where you will," ventured Douglass, "among black or white, [and they] must be looked up to—can never be looked down upon." Practiced by conscientious black people, such virtues could produce a formidable line of defense against racist detractors, for "in their presence, prejudice is abashed, confused and mortified. Encountering the solid mass of living character, our vile oppressors are ground to atoms."

Henry Highland Garnet, the redoubtable Presbyterian minister who never tired of speaking out against slavery, even going so far as to publicly call for a general slave uprising, also understood the use of virtue in the defense against racist hostilities. In his essay "The Past and the Present Condition and the Destiny of the Colored Race," he envisioned the conflict between the two races as somewhat like a fierce battle. "How shall we acquit ourselves on the field where the great battle is to be fought?" Garnet asked. His answer had all the earmarks of lauding the merits of the pursuit of virtue: "By following after peace and temperance, industry and frugality, and love to God, and to all men, and by resisting tyranny in the name of Eternal Justice."[17]

African American proponents of virtue understood the power inherent in the concept of temperance inasmuch as it denoted a level of mastery over warring impulses within the person. Slavery taught the slave to be submissive only to another; temperance admonished the free person to aspire to a mastery over the self, a mastery that if truly achieved would stand as a visible sign that such a person was truly free.

7

Virtue behind

the Veil of Secrecy

Stranger, allow me to inform you that the virtues
which should characterize a true St. Luke are honor, temperance,
faithfulness, obedience, meekness, charity, and brotherly
and sisterly kindness.

From the Ritual of the Independent Order of St. Luke, 1877

THE MANIFESTATIONS of the four cardinal virtues within the social consciousness of African Americans took shape within the arena of the general public. Significant venues in which virtue and its four manifestations were articulated were public gatherings, such as the meetings of the convention movement and protest rallies against injustices, and written material directed at the general public, such as editorials and essays.

There is yet another significant context in which the extolling of virtue was made, a context less open to public access, but no less important in shaping African American social consciousness in the nineteenth century. This context is one shrouded in secrecy—the fraternal societies and benevolent orders. Yet benevolent and fraternal secret orders functioned within a marginalized African American community as contexts in which notions of virtue could flourish and contribute to racial identity and uplift. Thus, virtue was nourished behind a veil of secrecy.

The Need for Secret Societies

On July 11, 1917, John E. Bush, one of the two founders of the benevolent secret society known as the Mosaic Templars of America,
was eulogized by one of the spiritual descendants of the first generation of that society, John Hamilton McConico. In a moving en-
comium to Bush, McConico affirmed that "three distinct causes gave
birth to the Templars: first, a white man's scorn, second, a Negro
woman's poverty, third, a Negro's shame."

Elaborating on the meaning of this cryptic reference to the
genesis of the society, McConico took his audience back to 1883
when Bush and a white man were talking on a street corner. An older
woman of color approached them, asking for assistance to bury her
husband. Both gave her something, after which the white man said,
"I cannot see or understand your race. When they throw their earnings away and whenever a Negro dies or needs help the public must
be worried to death by Negro beggars—it is a shame."

So stung was Bush by this insult that he called Chester W.
Keats and fifteen other black men and women together to form the
Mosaic Templars. Its original purpose was quite modest, intending
only to be a local benevolent and burial society, but it soon expanded
to eventually operate in twenty-six states. By 1924 it had more than
eighty thousand members nationwide with assets of more than
$300,000.[1]

During the latter years of the eighteenth century and throughout the nineteenth, when virtually all the benevolent, fraternal, and
secret societies among American blacks were formed, the central reasons for their founding were the same ones that occasioned the birth
of the Mosaic Templars. At the confluence of black economic need
and white contempt we may find the seeds for the birth of African
American benevolent orders. The collective reason for the formation
of the societies constituted a defiant response to the contempt in
which many whites held blacks. And to be sure, the history of many
of the societies reflected a pattern all too often discernible in American
history, that is to say, that of blacks forming their own benevolent societies when denied entrance to ones controlled by whites.[2]

African American secret benevolent orders have mitigated economic tenuousness by establishing a mutual aid contract among
their members and enforced the sociability within such groups with

the allure of secrecy and ritual. Sociologists have understood fraternal orders to designate a "variety of associations which combine secrecy and sociability with financial cooperation in meeting one or
more of the contingencies of life."[3] One could surmise that the allure
of secret societies involves an urge to construct a radical alternative
to the conventional world that constitutes daily, mundane activities.

Georg Simmel's insights on the nature of secret societies are useful here. Simmel observed that "the secret offers, so to speak, the possibility of a second world alongside the manifest world; and the latter
is decisively influenced by the former."[4] Simmel went on to suggest
that for the initiate into a secret society, its allure is heightened all the
more because the group offers a sense of freedom from the manifest
world: "The society lives in an area to which the norms of the environment do not extend" and holds out to its members a "sense of protection and confidence."[5] Thus, secret benevolent societies would offer
to black men—and women—the opportunity to participate in and
create a counterworld in which ethical ideals could be realized and,
above all, a world in which virtue could be inculcated and exemplified.

Secret fraternal orders among African Americans began during
the Revolutionary War period. The earliest one was the Masons,
founded by Prince Hall. Masonry, perhaps historically and still to this
day the most widespread fraternal order in the world, owes its existence
to medieval masons' guilds, which developed during the long period of
cathedral, monastery, and abbey building from the twelfth century on-
ward. Devoutly Christian, the guilds stressed fraternity, good works,
and the sacredness of the secret oath. Moreover, sociability, conviviality,
personal morality, equality, and peace were notable Masonic values.[6]

By the time of the English colonial settlements in North
America, Freemasonry had become a significant part of the English
culture. In England, Freemasonry found acceptance among the nobility and also among the rising middle and professional classes, who
saw within Masonry a spiritual home for their affinity to ideas such
as religious tolerance, free thinking, equality, and personal and civic
morality. On the Continent, however, Freemasonry had been either
under suspicion or outright denounced, as Pope Clement XII did in
a papal bull in 1738.

Carl Degler has reported that by 1741 Freemasonry had become
a part of the young American colonial cultural landscape.[7] It is not

surprising that the leading intellectual and cultural lights of the American Revolution, George Washington, General Lafayette, and Benjamin Franklin, were Masons. Nine signers of the Declaration of Independence and thirteen signers of the Constitution were Masons.[8]

The man who would become the founder of Freemasonry among blacks, Prince Hall, was probably born around 1735, place unknown, but appears in the historical record during the 1740s as the slave of William Hall of Boston. In the spring of 1770, the year of the Boston Massacre, Hall apparently gave Prince his freedom.

Prince Hall was one of a number of blacks in the Boston area who were caught up in the cause for American political freedom from Great Britain and in the cause of black liberation. Enterprising in spirit and a natural organizer by temperament, he seemed to have been a magnet to other black men who tried to counter the prevalent attitudes and customs against blacks at that time. There is evidence that he actively fought in the war. Others have stated that he fired a round at Bunker Hill. He also rendered service to the war effort as a skilled craftsman, documented by a bill he presented to Colonel Crafts of the Boston Regiment of Artillery on April 24, 1777, for five leather drumheads.[9]

As a race leader, an agitator for the rights of his people, and an advocate for the same principles of republican government and freedom from despotism against which other colonists were clamoring, Hall suffered two rebuffs in his efforts to act on those principles. For all of the Revolutionary rhetoric affirming the universal rights of man espoused by white patriots, there was no room in their world for black men to be accepted on a full and equal basis. The first rebuff occurred in 1775 when Hall addressed the Massachusetts Committee on Safety, urging the members of the committee to avail themselves of the ready store of black manpower ready to fight against England. Hall reasoned that the principles of equality and universal freedom, for which the colonists were willing to die in their revolt against England, ought to apply to the Africans and blacks within the colonists' midst. The committee was not to be persuaded. With John Hancock and Joseph Warren as members, it declined the offer from the blacks to bear arms in the defense of liberty.[10]

The second rebuff Hall suffered was in his attempts to become a member of the Free and Accepted Order of Masons. Hall and fourteen other free black men petitioned for admittance to the white Boston St. John's Lodge, the first Masonic lodge officially authorized by the mother lodge of England. They were refused. Denied membership by the Americans, the fifteen blacks eventually found a home within Masonry through the agency of an Irish regiment of the British forces anchored in Boston harbor—Lodge No. 441, Irish Registry, attached to the Thirty-eighth Foot Regiment. The Irish regiment took them in as fellow Masons on March 6, 1775.[11]

When their Irish patrons left the Boston area, Hall and his fellow Masons were accordingly left with limited power; they had a qualified permit to meet as a lodge. They could not, however, confer Masonic degrees or receive new members. A permanent charter would not be granted until after the war. Eventually, the grand master of the mother lodge of England, the duke of Cumberland, supported the Irish regiment's earlier action and issued a charter for the separate functioning of African Lodge No. 459. A charter, dated September 29, 1784, was personally delivered to Prince Hall by James Scott, a sea captain and the brother-in-law of the eminent John Hancock.[12]

The Advocacy of Black Freemasons

Soon after the granting of the charter, the black Freemasons became actively involved in the affairs of their particular ethnic community and offered, as circumstances turned out, to assist a community that had earlier spurned help from black men. In 1786, during Shay's Rebellion, Hall offered Governor Bowdoin the services of the lodge as soldiers to help maintain order. In a letter dated November 16, 1786, he stated, "We, by the Providence of God, are members of a fraternity that not only enjoins upon us to be peaceable subjects to the civil powers where we reside, but it also forbids our having concern in any plot or conspiracies against the state where we dwell."[13]

As Loretta Williams observed, the Prince Hall Masons have historically stressed their commitment to idealized American values: honesty, unselfishness, loyalty, patriotism, and friendship. But responsibilities and duties "owed to God, our neighbor and ourselves" were also of prime importance in manifesting Masonic commitment.[14] Saunders Redding stated, "The Boston lodge was wide awake on matters of general welfare" for the black community.[15]

In 1788, and on numerous other occasions, black Masons had to petition the state legislature on behalf of black men who were routinely lured onto vessels with promises of work and were subsequently sold into slavery. The signers of a petition to the state legislature decrying this practice, signed on February 27, 1788, were all members of African Lodge No. 459. Through their efforts, one such rescue of a kidnapped black man actually proved to be successful.

The education of black children was a particular concern of the black Masons. In 1786 Prince Hall, Lancaster Hill, Nero Brewster, and other Masons petitioned the Massachusetts legislature for educational facilities for black children.[16] The petition was denied, but in 1789, due to Masonic efforts, the first black public school in the United States was opened at No. 8 Smith Court in Boston.[17]

An influential black Masonic lodge was formed in Philadelphia in 1794 with Richard Allen, Absalom Jones, and James Forten Sr. among the leaders. The movement spread rapidly throughout the North and reached as far west as California with the gold rush of 1849. Restrictive legislation in the South made for great difficulties in organizing, but the movement thrived in Baltimore and the District of Columbia as early as 1825.[18]

In a moving farewell message to one of the newly planted African American lodges, Hall reminded his fellow Masons of the "noble order you are members of," urging them to "live up to the precepts of it, as you know that they are all good." He ended the message, "If thus we, by the grace of God, live up to this our profession, we may cheerfully go the rounds of the compass of this life, having lived according to the plumb-line of uprightness, the square of justice, the level of truth and sincerity."[19]

After an eventful life of service to his people and his community, forceful agitation for the rights of his people, and exertion for the ideal of freedom for a nation that often spurned his offer for aid, Prince Hall died in 1807. Hall's legacy to African Americans is not only the Masonic order that bears his name, that of Prince Hall Masons, but also a paradigm of a movement that could exemplify a quest for public virtue, moral purity, and race consciousness.

Subsequent to the rise of the Masons, throughout the nineteenth century there was a flourishing of benevolent and fraternal orders among blacks. The growth among northern blacks especially during the first half of the nineteenth century appears to be nothing short of phenomenal. W. E. B. DuBois reported that while Philadelphia alone had eleven benevolent societies in 1813, by 1838 that number had increased to one hundred, with a total of 7,448 members.[20] By 1902, when he wrote *The Story of the Negro,* Booker T. Washington could count at least twenty nationally prominent secret societies among African Americans.

The Order of Odd Fellows

Historically, perhaps the next significant secret society that came into being among African Americans was the Order of Odd Fellows. Significant also is that its genesis among blacks followed closely the same pattern as the one that marked the rise of Freemasonry among African Americans. An initial request from blacks for membership was spurned, after which a credentialing process with the aid of specially placed friends led to the first lodge among them being formed.

Begun in Europe, Odd Fellowship crossed the ocean to the United States in 1819 and soon began to grow on American soil. The Order of Odd Fellows become the first fraternal benefit order that African Americans joined. Its first African American lodge, the Philomathean, made its debut in New York City on March 1, 1843.[21] But the steps toward actual inclusion of blacks within this fraternal benevolent order were not without considerable pain and racial hostilities.

In 1842 the Philomathean Literary and Musical Society of New York, a club composed of free blacks, spurred by a "need for mutual aid and protection in case of sickness and distress," petitioned the Independent Order of Odd Fellows of New York for a dispensation and were refused. Spurned by the Americans, the blacks devised a plan of applying directly to the English mother lodge. Their plan met with success, principally through the efforts of Peter Ogden, a steward on a ship that sailed regularly between New York and Liverpool. Ogden, who would later be venerated as the father of Odd Fellowship among African Americans, managed to be initiated into the Victoria Lodge No. 448 in Leeds, England. Returning to the States, armed with the necessary credentials and documents, Ogden was able to help transform the Philomathean Society into Lodge No. 646 of the Grand United Order of Odd Fellows of America, on March 1, 1843.[22]

The overlay of the rituals of secrecy helped to transform an order that was in essence a benevolent mutual aid society into one that self-consciously viewed itself as having near religious and exalted status. The seal of the order carried a staff superimposed on an open book, underneath which were two hands clasped in a handshake, all of which was circumscribed by a serpent ingesting itself in a circular fashion with the motto "Amicitia, Amor et Veritas"—Friendship, Love and Truth—written underneath all of the symbols. Thus in a powerful way, significant elements of a life of virtue were set forth for the believer and member of the order: the open book depicting truth and the quest for prudence, the hands clasped as a symbol of just relations between people, a life tempered and moderated by friendship.

It is not surprising therefore that the Order of Odd Fellows regarded the date of the order's founding with an attitude that nearly resembled veneration. Ceremonies commemorating this date were replete with rhetoric and reflection worthy of the recounting of sacred history. Such an interpretation of past events managed to combine a due regard to virtue and the task of ensuring the viability and integrity of the race.

Charles B. Wilson, the author of a definitive book on the order, rose to the rank of deputy grand master by 1894. In reflecting on the founding date of the order, Wilson imagined that the principles of the lodge, "Friendship, Love and Truth," had through divine action been "promulgated to the American Negro."[23] The order would fancy itself a special harbinger of the lofty aspirations of African Americans; within its ranks would come forth men and women who would live out in exemplary ways the high ideals and virtue it promulgated.

When the order met for a biennial meeting in Cincinnati in 1884, the Rev. Benjamin W. Arnett gave the Biennial Oration before the gathering and viewed his audience as a veritable phalanx of his race in their quest for integrity: "As I look on this vast concourse of people representing in a large measure the intelligence, virtue, industry, and wealth of more than thirty states of the American Union, and the Dominion of Her Majesty the Queen, you are the legitimate representatives of more than three millions of men, women and children. To you we look for the moral, social and mutual well-being of the race."[24]

Arnett apparently saw no serious distinction between the values of the order and those of Christian faith, holding that all that he would offer in his oration would be in accordance with "the Fatherhood of God and the Brotherhood of Man as taught by Christian Ethics and Exemplified in the Grand United Order of Odd Fellows." For Arnett, natural religion was not sufficient in its power to provide an adequate basis for morals or ethics, or to "meet the demands of mankind." In his estimation, "Christian ethics is the only system that meets all the demands, for it is a system of morals, reached by scientific investigation of the moral consciousness of man, as enlightened, elevated, and purified by the Christian religion."[25]

The rule that bound the Odd Fellows together was the Golden Rule of Jesus: "As I would that men should do unto me, do I even so to them." Moreover, the order

> impresses the teachings of the word of God on our hearts. It makes us regard all men as our brethren. It drives away that mean and pusillanimous selfishness which has been the curse of society and the prison of so much greed. Our organization will break the chains that shut men up in their creeds and doctrines. It will empty their heads of so much self conceit; it will warm up their cold hearts, open their eyes to see the wants of their fellow man; and their pockets to relieve.[26]

Besides the fact that the order teaches "men to see the image of God in every situation in life," it "makes every man feel as though he was his brother's keeper, and therefore responsible to him for his actions." This concern for one's metaphorical "brother" was for Arnett a critical aspect of their organizing themselves. Against the detractors of mutual aid societies and those who scorned their rituals and ceremonies as a love of display and curiosity, he offered that their coming together was a positive response to the question put to Cain: "Where is your brother?" He declared, "That is why you have come to this place, to seek your brother of the order and of the race. We have come to see what we can do to assist in solving the unsolved Negro problem."[27]

Arnett went on to recite a sacred history of the Odd Fellows among African Americans, the lamentable tale of white exclusion, the anointed role of Peter Ogden and other founders, grandiloquently referred to as "the fathers of the Negro race." The founder of the movement among blacks was raised to a veritable messianic status:

> He [God], therefore, raised unto us a Moses in the person of Peter Ogden, who He destined to bring the Grand United Order of Odd Fellows to the outraged and helpless Negroes of America, to bless and cheer them in life, making them better husbands, kinder fathers and respectable citizens; teaching them the natural blindness of the human heart, and asking that they permit the holy truth, or Word of God, to remove the bandage from the eyes of the soul, and thereby enable them to walk with confidence and security; to enable them to better observe objects in their true and proper relations.[28]

He also viewed the sympathetic role played by the English Odd Fellows as providential:

> When our future was dismal and portentous; when our aspirations were divided and our manhood was denied; . . . we appealed to the Grand United Order in England for a charter. In hope and fear we waited for a response. The Christian enlightened spirit of fraternization from across the waters arose above the prejudice and injustice of our country. Hated as men and brethren, our gratitude, faithfullness, and love will endure to the end of time.[29]

He termed this experience "the night of our bondage" when England came and "lit up our pathway," "came to us when we were left as dead, with no rights that other humanity were bound to respect."

Thus having been formed and having inculcated all of the moral values and the mutual aid that were so much a part of the ethos and ethic of the movement, the lodge has "done more for the race than anything else outside of the Church of God," concluded Arnett.

The sacred history of race regeneration as interpreted by Arnett was echoed by Deputy Grand Master Wilson, who could write, after chronicling the struggles that Ogden and others endured to institute the order, "You will observe, dear brethren, that God, in His infinite goodness and mercy, did not intend that the hated and despised Negro in America should be deprived of this means of bettering his condition in life, elevating the character of each other, and teaching the principles of the Fatherhood of God and the brotherhood of man."[30]

The divine plan of which Wilson saw evidence in the near salvific work of Peter Ogden was to be augmented by the mutual support that each member of the order was bound to uphold. A practical purpose of the order was "for raising a fund for the relief of the members when sick, lame or disabled; and for insuring a sum of money to assist in defraying the expenses of burials, to be paid the widow, legal executors, administrators or assigns of a member deceased, or to assist in defraying the expense of the burial of the wife or child of a member."[31]

Arnett could see the practical consequences of ritual and ceremony and the importance of the notion of duty insofar as they would build a sense of moral community. While boasting that "we are a community within a community—an empire within an empire," he could go on to theorize how the order had contributed to a notion of racial cohesion by recognizing "that man is formed of so frail and brittle a material that he can only be held to his duty by the adamantine chain of obligation; if he doesn't feel obligated he'll throw it off on neighbors to visit the sick, bury the dead, etc." Furthermore, "if you can get him to kneel at the sacred altar and have him promise that he will, according to his ability, endeavor to perpetuate and strengthen the principles of mutual friendship, and that he will learn, practice and teach the fundamental principles of the order to his brother, and that he will always assist a worthy brother in distress, this will bind him like a chain."[32]

Secret Societies and Social Reform

Because social uplift was a prominent theme in their development, African American fraternal orders became involved with movements for general reform within U.S. society during the middle years of the nineteenth century. In the 1840s as the United States began to experience social stresses brought on by increased urbanization and industrialization, efforts for social betterment crystallized into what has been called the reform movement.

Notable among the social ills that the reformers sought to eradicate was the widespread use of strong drink and the abuse of alcohol. Thus, the temperance movement was born. It was aimed at mitigating some of the perceived social pathologies associated with undisciplined alcohol use, such as poverty, unstable family life, and the abuse of women and children.

African American proponents of the inculcation of virtue perceived within the reform movement efforts at social betterment that resonated to their concerns. After all, the very pathologies that the temperance movement sought to mitigate were anathema to the black community as well. African American proponents of virtue were determined that strong drink would not wreak havoc in their lives, homes, and communities. There was a concern that drunkenness could dissipate their energies, produce harmful public images, and generally erode the integrity of their communities.

In 1833 Rev. J. W. C. Pennington could write that "the Rum system, like that of slavery is upheld by ignorance, avarice and incorrect views of duty."[33] Benjamin Quarles estimated, for example, that at least one quarter of the black population of Cincinnati belonged to some kind of temperance society in the 1840s.[34] Given their assessment of the enormous challenges that stood in front of them and the debilitating effects strong drink could marshal to frustrate meeting those challenges, there was an understandable affinity between the temperance movement and efforts for black uplift.

The Independent Order of Good Samaritans

African Americans would eventually be drawn to and dominate a benevolent order that the temperance movement inspired—the Independent Order of the Good Samaritans and Daughters of Samaria. The order was organized on March 9, 1847, by Dr. Isaac Covert and others as a local temperance society in New York City. The focus was reforming alcoholics in New York's Bowery and Lower East Side. Its principles were the following:

> To carry forward the work of temperance reform, to secure sympathy and relief for the unfortunate and distressed families of those who pledge themselves to abstain from all intoxicating drinks, to elevate the living, to comfort the widow and fatherless in the hour of their affliction and

bury the dead of our Order. And it is the enjoined duty of all to watch over one another in sickness and in health and to remonstrate with those who wander from the paths of rectitude and sobriety.[35]

Despite the lofty tone and the implied social inclusiveness inherent in its principles, the Order of the Good Samaritans was initially organized on a racially segregated basis; blacks were admitted, but were organized into separate units and were allowed to vote only on matters concerning them. Whites were organized in state lodges, blacks in district lodges. Six months after the founding of the order, the first grand lodge was organized on September 14. Women were admitted when the first lodge of the Daughters of Samaria was organized on December 9, 1847. At the first meeting of the grand lodge, a charter was granted to J. W. B. Smith, a black man, to organize Fountain Lodge No. 1 and to organize other black people into lodges.[36]

Apparently, racial tension dogged each step of the growth of the order. In this respect the order was typical of other movements that began in the middle years of the nineteenth century. In his study of benevolent orders and movements from this period, *Fifty Million Brothers,* William Ferguson documents the typical pattern of initial white resistance to acceptance of blacks on an equal basis and the subsequent racial tensions.[37] In this respect, the Order of the Good Samaritans and Daughters of Samaria was typical. But the dynamics were such that eventually within the order, blacks would dominate it after whites abandoned it when faced with increasing numbers of blacks joining the movement.

Electoral politics and racial animosity seemed to play a major role in the eventual ascendancy of African Americans in the order. In 1881, the inability to reconcile arguments over the construction of an Asylum for Inebriates led to the formation of three national branches, each claiming to be the true and legitimate one. The union of two of these branches, combined with the increase of black membership, resulted in the election of a black grand sire in 1887. The corresponding decrease in white membership meant that by that time the order had become for all practical purposes an African American organization.[38]

In 1881, well before African Americans would come to political ascendancy within the organization, but sometime after he had been elected a grand chief of District Lodge No. 3 in Washington, D.C., an administrative unit reserved for blacks, Howard H. Turner sat down to write his version of the history of the Good Samaritans. Availing himself of some theological license, Turner averred that the very name of the order—Samaritans—recognized the general history of apostasy and idolatry practiced by the ancient Samaritans. However, his hope was that as their modern-day descendants, they would act with more moral rectitude. In his history he pleaded with blacks to order their lives in conformity with virtue and to remain free from the curse of drunkenness.[39]

Grand United Order of True Reformers

Yet another secret society that managed to combine zeal for the temperance movement, moral regeneration, and economic uplift for African Americans was the Grand United Order of True Reformers, formed under the leadership of the charismatic personality of Rev. William Washington Browne. Browne was born a slave in Habersham County, Georgia, on October 20, 1849. At age eight he was taken to Rome, Georgia, and from there was sold to a plantation in west Tennessee, about nine miles from Memphis. There he remained until the outbreak of the Civil War. He escaped to Union lines outside Memphis sometime during 1863, attaching himself to the Sixth Missouri Regiment as a serving boy and later performing other duties in the Union army. Upon discharge from the Union army, Browne attended school in Prairie-du-Chien, Wisconsin.

After the war he returned to Georgia to accept a teaching position. As a man of some education he received immediate respect from the black community. That reputation was enhanced even more through his speaking out against the terrorist tactics used by the Ku Klux Klan. But Browne not only attacked the tactics of intimidation used by the Klan; he also regarded alcohol as a social nemesis for black people. He argued that "king alcohol" killed or disabled a disproportionate number of blacks, pointing out to audiences that blacks convicted of public drunkenness usually ended up on the chain gang, suffered loss of earning power, and eventually became disfranchised. Browne believed that the political and economic consequences associated with alcohol were so dire that an all-out offensive against liquor was warranted.

Desiring access to the resources of an already established organization, Browne sought the endorsement of a local white temperance society in Alabama to gain credentials to form an organization among blacks in Georgia. The Alabama group, the Good Templars of Alabama, was the state agent of the Independent Order of Good Templars of the World. In 1873 the Alabama chapter offered him a deal: he would receive a charter and sponsorship but only under a separate name, as the United Order of True Reformers. Browne accepted the compromise and in 1874 quit his teaching position to devote his full energies to temperance and the United Order of True Reformers. By the next year he had founded enough local chapters, or "subfountains," to establish a "Grand Fountain" in accordance with instructions from the Good Templars. This achievement was no mean testimony to Browne's organizational skill and crusading zeal—and to the power the temperance message held in black communities—for the Good Templars required the creation of fifty subfountains before a Grand Fountain could be formed.[40]

Browne was a tireless speaker and advocate of temperance, even under the racially exclusive circumstances imposed by the Good Templars. But he and other blacks soon chafed under the conditions and set out to make plans to form an autonomous African American organization. Finally settling in Richmond, Virginia, in 1875, he observed several benevolent and burial societies for blacks and saw in them the model he needed. Moreover, temperance lodges outnumbered all other black organizations in the city. Through loyalty and contacts he had been able to establish through his work with the Good Templars, he succeeded in bringing many groups together in 1876 to form the Grand Fountain of True Reformers, headquartered in Richmond with himself as grand worthy master. Because of his charismatic leadership and organizational prowess, the group had attracted more than five thousand members by 1878, organized into forty-five local units, or fountains.[41]

Under Browne's leadership, the Grand United Order of True Reformers formed a bank and an insurance company, existing side by side. The Savings Bank of the Grand Fountain, United Order of True Reformers, was established in March 1888. According to Carter G. Woodson, the Savings Bank became such a strong institution that during the panic of 1893, it managed to pay all claims presented to it when other banks in the city of Richmond had to refuse. During the first twenty-three years of the Savings Bank, its assets reached $500,000 with ten thousand depositors, doing a volume of business exceeding $10,000,000. It was the first black-owned and black-operated bank chartered in the United States. The insurance feature of the organization paid out sick benefits, and upon their deaths holders of policies could leave a substantial sum for their dependents.[42]

Browne's motto and vision statement in all of his work was "combination, concentration and cooperation," ideals he expounded upon constantly in his newspaper, *The Reformer*. In accordance with those three aims, he set up a virtual economic conglomerate involving a real estate department, a commercial department with a chain of stores, and a home for elderly persons. The goal of the entire organization went beyond the sole accumulation of wealth; it sought to "break down crime, licentiousness, poverty and wretchedness" while promoting "happiness, peace, plenty, and protection."[43]

Other Secret Societies

Besides the Odd Fellows and the Good Samaritans, the years immediately prior to the Civil War saw the births of several other national secret organizations that were dedicated to African American liberty and the propagation of virtue. John Hope Franklin notes the conspicuous roles played in African American life by groups such as the Friendship Benevolent Society for Social Relief, the Star in the East Association, and the Daughters of Jerusalem in a city like Baltimore, for example.

Often coming together in the face of hostile white sentiments, groups such as the Band Society of New Orleans, a group of free black artisans, could organize themselves, as they did in 1860, under the motto "Love, Union, Peace." In addition to meeting together over matters of mutual concern with regard to their commercial interests, they admonished one another "to go about once in a while and see one another in love" and to wear the society's regalia on special occasions.[44] The themes and mottoes of benevolent and secret orders were always consistent with those of the black churches, in which members of the orders were also active.

The very names of orders are redolent with religious ideas and even biblical lore: the Grand and United Order of Galilean Fishermen, the Nazarites, and the Seven Wise Men. The combination of interest in ancient mystery cults and in Christian religion could produce a group such as the Knights of Wise Men, founded either during or immediately after the Civil War. The order was of the firm belief that it stood for or taught nothing "that can conflict with the most sacred duties. On the contrary, it seeks to enforce those duties which, in the hardening struggle of life, men are too prone to forget." At some point during each meeting or ritual of the Knights of Wise Men, members must have taken immense pride in singing the opening ode to the tune of "Auld Lang Syne":

> *How truly blessed is the sight*
> *of Knights assembled here*
> *Who in each other's peace delight*
> *And soothe each other's care.*
>
> *Who each his brother's failings hide*
> *'Neath true fraternal love,*
> *And free from selfish, jealous pride,*
> *By works their faith do prove.*[45]

Particularly noteworthy in terms of alleged exploits, if legend is true, was the International Order of Twelve, Knights and Daughters of Tabor. Moses Dixon, a free-born barber and minister, professed to have founded in 1846 a secret society among the slaves called the Knights of Liberty for the avowed purpose of forcibly destroying slavery. Dixon declared that the Knights of Liberty had branches in every southern state except Missouri and Texas, and that by 1856 "the army of true and trusted men numbered 47,240 Knights of Liberty."[46] Dixon's claims of this massive clandestine army cannot be verified. He might have invented the story to give realism to the ritual of the order that he formally established after the war in 1871. The existence of such a group is cast somewhat in doubt by his further claim that all of the Knights were killed in the Civil War except himself. He also declined to divulge the secrets or rolls of the Knights of Liberty to "safeguard" the descendants of its members against reprisals.[47]

But whether an actual brilliant military leader or the stuff of heroic legend, Dixon, a larger-than-life personage, struck a chord in the imagination of his followers. As late as 1920 the spirit and ideas of race uplift and virtue inherent in the International Order of Twelve, Knights and Daughters of Tabor were still alive.

Addressing the spiritual descendants of the original Twelve at their Eighteenth Grand Session in Macon, Georgia, Chief Grand Mentor Dr. Edwin J. Turner told the gathered assembly: "Our order is the outgrowth of the sufferings, torments, and hardships of a helpless people, a race that was kept in bondage for two hundred and fifty years, slaves of a race that mocked God. . . . Our mission in life is one of charity and mercy, and regardless of what the enemy says we must not divert one iota from the duty imposed upon us."[48]

Striking a defiant tone that must have been reminiscent of the daring Dixon, Dr. Turner went on to recount in a capsulized form his vision of how his order came to represent the history and destiny of African Americans:

> When we impress upon them [prospective members or skeptics] the fact that ours is the outgrowth of a real negro's brain; when we tell them of how Moses Dixon tramped up and down the Mississippi River in the days of slavery and how his heart bled with grief because of the sufferings of our forefathers by the overseer's lash; when we tell them how he saw our mothers and fathers and their children torn apart and placed upon the auction block; when we tell them how he creeped around in the darkness from one plantation to another to organize the Knights of Liberty they readily glean that Tabor has a real foundation and that this Order is just as dear to the negro as the Knights of Columbus is to the Catholics and the Ku Klux Klan is the Southern white man. We have principles and traditions to preserve for a race just as they have.[49]

The Colored Knights of Pythias, formed in 1870, was another secret order that came to exemplify the celebration of virtue combined with racial solidarity and uplift. Its formation would parallel the racial dynamics that played so conspicuous a role in prior secret orders among blacks, notably, for example, the Masons and the Odd Fellows.

The idea for the Knights of Pythias was conceived in 1864 by a man named Justus H. Rathbone, a federal government clerk in Washington, D.C., who had an intense and long-standing interest in ancient mystery cults. Gifted with dramatic and theatrical flair, he had been engaged in amateur dramatics and was greatly moved by the ideology of a play of the period called *Damon and Pythias,* by John Banim. He later wrote a lodge ritual based on the Pythagorean philosophy and notions of eternal friendship as embodied in the play. In 1864, he attempted to found a secret order based on his ideas and interest in antiquity, but a year later it was defunct. Intent on successfully founding an order based on his ideas, he revived the ritual, and by 1868 the lodge had grown to three thousand. While they had a limitation to "Caucasian," Jews were admitted.[50] Blacks were categorically excluded from membership.

Shortly after its founding some sympathetic whites tried to intervene on behalf of some black men who had shown an interest in the lodge. At a supreme lodge meeting in New York on March 8, 1870, a petition was presented by four white men on behalf of black men in Philadelphia for an order. The petition was summarily turned down. That event, however, shrouded as it was in white arrogance and rejection of black desires to be a part of the movement, affirmed universal betterment and the quest for virtue. African American chroniclers of the order would remember the event and cast it in decidedly theological terms: "Divine Providence had willed that the colored men should not be denied the lessons of uplift as taught in the Pythian Brotherhood."[51]

Eventually, using a combination of intrigue, stealth, and persistence, a lodge under the supervision of blacks was formed. The chroniclers of the birth of the Colored Knights of Pythias wrote that subsequent to this denial, "certain who appeared to be of the other race [white], led by George A. Place of Macon, Miss., Dr. Thomas W. Stringer of Vicksburg, Miss., A. E. Lightfoot of Lauderdale, Miss. were initiated into the Order."[52] They then proceeded to initiate and form an order for blacks. Another theory holds that several black men who could pass for white infiltrated the lodge, gained the necessary secret lore relative to ceremony, and subsequently formed a lodge for blacks.

We may never know the true circumstances surrounding the origin, but the Colored Knights of Pythias became an organization that was unabashedly sensitive to the aspirations and needs of African Americans. The dedication to a handbook of this branch of the lodge encapsulated critical components of virtue: the development of the enlightened mind and prudence, the establishment of justice. The dedication read in part:

> To each loyal knight, battling for racial self-help through the dissemination of the principles of Friendship, Charity and Benevolence; to each Sir Knight sworn to protect the Honor of the home circle, to seek justice for his brother and teach Loyalty to one another; to each Sister of Calanthe obligated under the banner of Friendship, Harmony and Love: to each Pythian Cadet being taught the lessons of Truth, Honor and Virtue, and to each Juvenile whose mind is led into the paths of Love, Kindness and Obedience.[53]

The Good of Secret Societies

At the end of the nineteenth century several notable observers confirmed the tremendous impact the mutual aid, benevolent, and secret societies had made on the cultural and economic lives of African Americans. Booker T. Washington, in writing *The Story of the Negro*, devoted an entire chapter to such societies. In assessing the abiding value of the fraternal orders among black people Washington affirmed that

> the chief value of the Negro societies and benevolent organizations has been that they have been the schools in which the masses have been taught the value and the methods of cooperation. In order to succeed these organizations have been compelled to enforce upon the masses of the people habits of saving and of system which they would not otherwise have been able or disposed to learn. These societies have contributed in this way, in spite of their failings, in no small degree to the intellectual and material development of the Negro race.[54]

As a man of considerable entrepreneurial spirit, Washington took pride in noting the economic strength that benevolent orders brought to the black community. He mentioned the impressive office buildings that had been erected by the Odd Fellows in Philadelphia, by the Knights of Pythias in Chicago and New Orleans, each costing $100,000.[55]

Throughout the nineteenth century the mutual aid and secret societies among African Americans provided the context where virtue could be pursued within the confines of fraternal benevolence and the rituals of secrecy. Well into the twentieth century they served the same purpose. In an address before the Grand Temple and Tabernacle of the Georgia Jurisdiction of the International Order of Twelve, Knights and Daughters of Tabor, meeting in Valdosta, Georgia, in 1921, Chief Grand Mentor Dr. Edwin J. Turner admonished his audience with the following: "Therefore . . . I say, love knowledge with a great love; love innocence; love virtue; love purity of conduct; love that which, if you are rich and great, will sanctify the providence which has made you so."[56] Such was, and is, the legacy of the earlier luminaries who were convinced that virtue could, indeed, flourish behind the veil of secrecy.

8

VIRTUE AND
THE PROMISE FOR
A NEW PEOPLE

◼

All we had was freedom.

Anonymous Freedman after the Civil War

WHEN THE GUNS of the Civil War were silenced in the spring of 1865, four and a half million persons of African descent were finally freed from bondage. They doubtless believed that their prayers and the hopes of their ancestors who had died in bondage had at long last been vindicated. They also surely believed that the relentless activism of many other black people and, as the nation came to struggle with itself in a bloody Civil War, the presence of at least 180,000 men of their own color in Union blue had brought the day of Jubilee to pass.

Without question, the first and second generations of black people who gained maturity as free men and women after the Civil War saw themselves in a fortuitous and special light. They would be the harbingers of all the potential of the race, released from the confines of slavery, free to allow latent gifts to be fully developed. They would be born in freedom, could mature in freedom, and could, according to the visions of their forebears, live out their lives in the pursuit of virtue in freedom.

In what ways did the first and second generations of African Americans after the end of slavery articulate notions of virtue? How did they view such notions within the context of their struggle for race uplift and integrity? Virtue for them held out a hope of promise for a new people. This chapter will show that the collective voices of the African American church and the intellectual establishment, or the academy, worked together to keep the vision of virtue alive as African Americans entered a new century.

Virtue in the First Postbellum Generation

The generation of African Americans that could begin to breathe the air of freedom sensed the monumental challenges that awaited them as they sought to lead their lives as free people. The generations of slavery endured by them and their forebears were not designed to encourage the inculcation of personal skills, attitudes, and habits that could undergird life as free persons. Slavery was not an institution in which the mind could be enlightened; no honing of the virtue of prudence was possible within its shadowy constraints. The daily extraction of unearned bread by a captive's labor made a mockery of justice. Owned by another, the slave could not know the quiet dignity of self-possession and the meaning of living one's life in an ordered fashion, as temperance would have it.

As they assessed the daunting task of building full and virtuous lives in the aftermath of slavery, they echoed men such as Frederick Douglass and Austin Steward, who understood how difficult it was to inculcate virtue under the demoralizing conditions of slavery. Professor W. H. Crogman, a native of St. Martin and for years a professor of classics at Clark College in Atlanta, took this view thus: "When . . . I consider by what processes, during two centuries, the moral groundwork of my people was undermined and shaken, it is to me no wonder that many of them are to-day found immoral. The greater wonder is that their moral perception has not been entirely swept away."[1] Slavery, thought Crogman, "was a school ill adapted to the producing of pure and upright characters." He asked, "Can you rob a man continually of his honest earnings and not teach him to steal? Can you ignore the sanctity of marriage and the family relation and not inculcate lewdness? Can you constantly govern a man with the lash and expect him always to speak truth?"

As late as 1913 when he made a study of the social habits of blacks, W. E. B. DuBois, who would become the first systematic compiler and investigator of African American life toward the end of the nineteenth century, also condemned the effects of slavery on the moral life of many African Americans. He and one of his students, Augustus Dill, edited a publication entitled *Manners and Morals Among Negro Americans,* which was issued in conjunction with the Eighteenth Annual Atlanta University Conference. DuBois and Dill soberly reported that in addition to racial prejudice "the persistence of older habits due to slavery" was a very real inhibitor in the path of advance of the race. "It is not to be expected," they felt, "that a people whose original morality had been destroyed by slavery and but partially replaced should not show in a single generation of freedom many marks of the past in sexual irregularity, waste, irresponsibility and criminal tendencies."[2]

But lest any unsympathetic critics of blacks discern in such social and moral imperfections a reason to assign perpetual inferior status to them, Crogman advised that if such persons looked within their own race, given its advantages, no reason would be found for boasting. In referring to such critics, Crogman said, "They require among us, in twenty short years, a state of moral rectitude which they themselves, with far more favorable opportunities, have not reached in one hundred times twenty."[3]

The debilitating effects of slavery and its aftermath notwithstanding, the sons and daughters of recently freed blacks resolved that they would not allow the effects of slavery to reach into their generation, to eviscerate their moral lives, as slavery itself had attempted to do to their forebears. There was hope of building lives anew even in the aftermath of such a monstrous institution. Nothing could prevent it.

The aspirations of that first generation of freed blacks were certainly echoed in the opening words of a little pamphlet written by Isaac Brinckerhoff, a white abolitionist who before the war had worked with the American Tract Society and who became enlisted in the Freedmen's Aid enterprise early in 1862 as a teacher on the South Carolina Sea Islands. His *Advice to Freedmen* began with a direct salutation: "My friend, you was [*sic*] a slave. You are now a freedman." Brinckerhoff acknowledged that "though you have for generations been a dependent and enslaved race, . . . there is evidence of a God-given manhood within."[4] The belief in this "God-given manhood," or divinely sanctioned black humanity, would persuade the proponents of virtue in the generations after slavery that the quest for virtue should not cease.

Subsequent Generations in Church and Academy

At the end of the nineteenth century and as the new twentieth century was unfolding, vocal and persuasive spokespersons within the African American community representing the church as well as the academy joined together in affirming the quest for virtue. They would continue an exposition of the notion of character, the aspect of virtue without which Nathaniel Paul and Frederick Douglass had advised even freedom would be meaningless. Proponents of virtue—from church and academy, often straddling both worlds—thus continued a tradition forged in the first half of the nineteenth century as they sought to discern special ways in which virtue and character could ensure the general uplift of African Americans in the new century.

It may be safely said that the African American church—manifested across the denominational spectrum—has been the most central social institution in the life and culture of that community. For the proponents of virtue to argue that the churches among African Americans were critical to the inculcation of character and virtue among them, the proposition had to be affirmed regarding the centrality of the black church to black life and culture.

Among the many observers who intuitively affirmed the role and power of the black churches to inculcate a sustained life of virtue was the sociologist and historian W. E. B. DuBois. DuBois was responsible for what came to be perhaps the first systematic analysis of church life among African Americans. In *The Negro Church,* a 1903 study he compiled while at Atlanta University, he documented how the church provided immeasurable value as a source for social services to blacks and a context for social intercourse. It was central to the lives of African Americans. Its legitimacy as a social organization had an organic vitality to it; it was not an institution that had been grafted onto the community from other traditions or cultures. In this regard, DuBois could appreciate the African roots of the American black church. Said he in the frontispiece of the 1903 study:

> The Negro church is the only social institution of the
> Negroes which started in the African forest and survived
> slavery; under the leadership of priest or medicine man, af-
> terward of the Christian pastor, the Church preserved in
> itself the remnants of African tribal life and became after
> emancipation the center of Negro social life. So that today

the Negro population of the United States is virtually di-
vided into church congregations which are the real units of
race life.[5]

Most of the black commentators on African American religion
during this period would agree with DuBois's assessment. Bishop A.
Grant, who provided some of the data for the DuBois study, declared that the "church would be a decided misfit and a pronounced
failure if it finds itself other than a center." And for DuBois, because
the church allegedly assumed many of the social functions that had
been the responsibility of other social institutions, now shrouded in
the African past, "the Church became the center of amusements, of
what little spontaneous economic activity remained, of education,
and all social intercourse." Rev. W. H. Holloway, a minister who also
collaborated with the DuBois research team by providing a picture
of the religious life of blacks in Thomas County, Georgia, ventured
to say that a black person looks to the church "not only for his spiritual wants, but looks toward it as the center of his civilization."[6]

But the assertion that the black church played a critical role in
the social life of its members did not preclude its powerful spiritual
function as well. Through its preaching and religious services, it could
organize and shape the urgings the people had for a "word from God."

The DuBois volume itself warned against a superficial judgment that the church, even the rude, rural church, served a purely
social function. While DuBois and his collaborators allowed that it
was true that "the rally of the country churches, called the 'big meeting,' is the occasion for the pleasantest social intercourse, with a free
barbeque; and the Sunday-school convention and the various
preachers' conventions are occasion of reunions and festivities, one
must not hastily form the conclusion that the religion of such
churches is hollow or their spiritual influence bad. While under present circumstances the Negro church can not be simply a spiritual
agency, but must also be a social, intellectual, and economic center,
it *nevertheless* is a spiritual center of wide influence" (italics added).

Standing squarely in the center of this "spiritual center of wide
influence" was the black preacher. DuBois captured the essence of
this powerful figure in this lyrical description: "The Preacher is the
most unique personality developed by the Negro on American soil.
A leader, a politician, an orator, a 'boss,' an intriguer, an idealist—all

these he is."[7] At the same time, the black preacher was more than likely the most articulate person and, with other black professionals, among the better-educated people in the community, especially if the minister led a congregation of substantial size. By virtue of his position within the most central social institution in the black community, the black minister was bound to exert tremendous influence as one who could articulate issues concerning the destiny of the race.

Besides the figure of the minister as a spokesman for race matters, the academic assumed an increasingly important role in the latter years of the nineteenth century. Toward the end of that century the first graduates of the schools that had been founded primarily for blacks freed after the Civil War began to demonstrate their abilities as race leaders. They and their teachers, black men and women as well, had been steeped in industrial and classical education and felt a deep desire to chart the course for the race's future.

In the vision and articulation of steps toward race integrity and social uplift, theological ideas from the world of the clerics and intellectual concepts celebrated by the academics came together to form a view of the role of virtue in race progress. There is perhaps no greater symbol of this collaboration of church and academy than the founding of the American Negro Academy in 1898, under the leadership of Rev. Alexander Crummell, the rector of St. Luke's Episcopal Church in Washington, D.C. Crummell had seen the need for a group of intellectuals who could act as a counterweight to the materialism perceived in the philosophy of Booker T. Washington. But Crummell was not interested merely in the establishment of an esoteric debating society; he desired a forum of thinkers who could address the real issues facing African Americans at that time. Within the group, clergy such as Archibald Grimké and Crummell could discuss issues with academics such as Kelly Miller of Howard University and W. S. Scarborough of Wilberforce.

African American race leaders reflected on the moral imperatives inherent in life in freedom after slavery. Both clerics and intellectuals were brought together in a common enterprise of discerning how black people could best secure a measure of social and moral integrity in American life. Virtue could provide the undergirding structure for the total fabric of the responsible life. Alexander Crummell had sounded the theme in an 1885 address he gave to the graduating class at Storer

College when he said, "What we need is a grand *moral* revolution which shall touch and vivify the inner life of a people . . . which shall bring to them a resurrection from inferior ideas and lowly ambitions."[8]

Crummell's entire social philosophy was, it could be argued, a full exposition of the role of virtue in African American life. As an elaboration of what he meant when he called for a moral revolution, he let it be known that he had character clearly in mind. "The basis of this revolution must be character," he said. "*That* is the rock on which this whole race in America is to be built up."

Crummell saw that the active leadership role of enlightened and educated persons, who had developed a needed measure of prudence and foresight, was absolutely critical to the race's ability to progress. In the Storer College speech of 1885 he affirmed that "the rising intelligence of this race, the educated thinking . . . men, who come out of the schools trained and equipped by reading and culture," will be able to assume forceful leadership. Their leadership would be sorely needed to enable the race to fight against injustice, particularly in the struggle to deflect attempts at "defrauding black labor."

In his inaugural address as the first president of the American Negro Academy on March 5, 1897, Crummell again affirmed his view that leadership of the race ought to be reserved for those who had acquired training and a sense of prudence. Rejecting the idea that property and/or blood lineage are the sources of power and progress, Crummell averred that "the greatness of peoples springs from their ability to grasp the grand conceptions of being. It is the absorption of a people, of a nation, of a race, in large majestic and abiding things which lifts them up to the skies. These once apprehended, all the minor details of life follow in their proper places."[9] While Crummell believed that scholars and thinkers were to be the ones to lift the race to "the height of noble thought, grand civility, a chaste and elevating culture," he thought that such persons ought to be motivated "with a spirit of disinterestedness"[10] and go about their work in that fashion.

In Crummell's expectations of "disinterestedness," with its implied mastery over temptations to be unduly influenced by money, wealth, and power, we may discern a hint of the notion of temperance. Temperance for Crummell connoted the ability to hold mastery over oneself, to be self-possessed. He envisioned a quality of life for black people in which character could eventuate in such self-control. Speaking to a graduating class in 1884, he hoped that his young listeners would ultimately acquire "that training by which the intellectual forces are harmoniously developed, and reason and imagination are given their rightful authority. I mean the discipline which enables one to command his own powers, and then to use them with ease and facility."[11]

Crummell certainly intuited the need for fortitude if the leaders of the race, and the race itself, were to reach the desired levels of excellence he had projected. To struggle successfully against injustice, he told men of the Garnet Lyceum at Lincoln University, "You must have strength!"[12]

Rev. Francis J. Grimké, the brother of Archibald, and a colleague of Crummell in the American Negro Academy who would serve as a president of the group, reflected Crummell's social philosophy with respect to virtue but managed to present an even sharper rebuke to the attempts to politically marginalize black people at that time. A sermon published by the American Negro Academy in 1905, entitled "The Negro and His Citizenship," made it clear that he was not about to compromise in the matter of the push for political rights. Grimké confessed that "I belong to what may be called the radical wing of the race, on the race question: I do not believe in compromises; in surrendering, or acquiescing, even temporarily, in the deprivation of a single right, out of deference to an unrighteous public sentiment."[13] In fact, for Grimké, compromising on the issue of rights would be tantamount to vitiating any moral integrity the race would have developed as a result of acquiring character. He believed, quoting the poet James Russell Lowell, that "They enslave their children's children, Who make compromise with sin."

Clerics and academics alike in the phalanx of black leadership affirmed that God has created a just moral universe. Moreover, through disciplining the powers of the intellect, human beings may be able to discern the proper ways and avenues for productive and responsible living in society. Those who will have acquired such an ability will have acquired a sense of character, a life ordered in such a way that social, moral, and material progress will be assured. Such are the aspects of virtue that race leaders articulated in the closing years of the nineteenth century and the beginning years of the twentieth.

Discerning a Godly Place in Society

Proponents of African American virtue at century's end believed in their place in a morally just universe. It is not an overstatement to suggest that the generation of black leaders who rose to prominence after the Civil War and before the turn of the twentieth century were obsessed with the determination to find a place for themselves and their people within U.S. society and the wider moral universe as well. Such a place was in stark contrast to the continuing constrictions imposed upon the race in the aftermath of the war and the end of Reconstruction. They were imbued with a sense of place in a just and moral universe superintended by God.

One is tempted to suggest that such a vision, based as it was on metaphysically deep and enduring principles, was of great functional value in an era when the worth of blacks was challenged with oppressive regularity. For his part, Rev. Edward Brawley could actually affirm that "the young Negro is turning his social and political disadvantages to his best interest by relying calmly upon the justice and wisdom of God's moral government. Life is, indeed, but a conflict of forces, but the intelligent young Christian Negro knows that the universe does not operate by chance."[14]

Years earlier, Archibald Grimké had affirmed the belief that the moral universe was governed by a just mind. In editing a Boston weekly called the *Hub* from 1883 to 1885 he sounded an essentially transcendentalist theme, much like that of Hosea Easton and others some fifty years earlier. Human society, he opined, was fundamentally governed by an ultimate moral force:

> In its last analysis, civil society rests upon force—but this force is moral, not physical. . . . The visible is transient—individual and corporeal—and as a cause, must in the nature of things be secondary. The invisible is eternal, impersonal, moral, and as cause, is beneath, in and above the merely visible, and, so far as it is concerned, ranks as primary. . . . The world is governed by mind.[15]

W. H. Crogman offered what may be considered a credo for his life's work and an example of this vision:

> In the face of these divergences, in the face of these misgivings and doubts—many of them honest—I am still in-

clined to range myself on the side of those who believe that life is a blessing, that it is beneficent in design, that it is governed by laws as unchangeable as those that govern the planets, and that by a close and diligent study into its deeper and hidden meanings, we may not only live it successfully but even rise superior to many of those things which are commonly called its ills and annoyances and disappointments.[16]

A divinely ordered and just moral universe mitigates the seeming inequities experienced in life. In this regard, William A. Sinclair, in his book *The Aftermath of Slavery*, could declare, "God has a purpose in every soul He sends into the world. The poorest, most helpless infant is not an accident, a few molecules of matter, merely, but a plan of God, and as such deserves to be trained for its work. Every child has a right to a chance in life because God made him and made him to do something."[17]

Both Crogman and Sinclair suggest in these very moving statements that the structures that obtain in the workaday world of men and women in society have integrity and purpose by virtue of their grounding in the enduring world of principles superintended by God. Crogman's classicism and celebration of the intellect convinced him that this link between these two worlds awaited discovery and exploration by the inquisitive and prepared mind. For Crogman, the reflective and disciplined mind is provided entrance into the good life by delving into the nature of God's natural and moral universe. Said Crogman, "The book of nature is as much God's book as the book of revelation. In fact, they are both a revelation, and were both meant to be read as a help to meditation, to devotion, to cheerful living."[18]

To attain a modicum of "cheerful living," in Crogman's words, or certainly a level of race integrity in the grander scheme of life in the United States, the proponents of virtue affirmed that the enlightened mind could discern mandates from the moral universe about how to conduct life. Rev. Francis J. Grimké, who was freed after the war and eventually graduated from Princeton Theological Seminary, would preach to his congregation and others his belief that human beings were endowed with the capacity to penetrate the world of "mind" by which God has designed the moral universe.

As pastor of Washington's Fifteenth Street Presbyterian Church for more than a half century, Grimké affirmed a doctrine of humanity that celebrated moral autonomy and human responsibility. In his sermons he voiced the opinion that every person was a "rational creature, a free moral agent, a responsible being, and therefore God's method of dealing with him is different."[19] And good consequences could ensue from using reason. Such a mind, if it acquired the ability to reflect deeply on the nature of being, could begin to fathom the host of problems that confronted human beings in society. Crogman too affirmed the role of discernment in achieving moral responsibility. In 1895, in a baccalaureate address to the graduates of Clark College entitled "Life's Deeper Meanings," he articulated this:

> As finite beings we shall, of course, never be able to foresee all things, nor make adequate provision for all contingencies. Yet it is nonetheless true, that we often blame one another, blame society, blame government, blame the Almighty himself for afflictions and calamities, both personal and national, which might have been averted by the exercise of forethought on our part, or by little deeper investigation into the nature of things.[20]

Clearly, Crogman believed that sobriety and forethought were necessary characteristics of the well-ordered life of temperance.

To Crogman, such sobriety was not a source of drudgery. Rather, "far from imposing life upon us as a burden, God evidently intended life to be a constant delight." There was for Crogman a creative tension between such delight and serious service rendered to God, between freedom and structure. "God intended us," he declared, "to be free in the broadest possible sense of the term, in order that we might render to Him cheerful service. Freedom is, indeed, the first condition requisite to voluntary heart service; for no man living or laboring under a sense of drudgery, under a sense of burden, could possibly exclaim with the Psalmist: 'I delight to do thy will, O God'" (Ps. 40:8 KJV).[21]

The temperate life, undergirded by this link between the world of principles and the world of workaday affairs, was also articulated by Rev. George Gilbert Walker, who could in 1909 believe that the race was yet in a formative stage. Hence out of a call for urgency he declared that "we must make emphatic our progress in the essentials of the higher life. Rather than pay too much attention to insignificant and non-essential things, we must be sedulous in working out important principles and essential things."[22]

Crogman, although a classics scholar, could still use biblical imagery (with a faint trace of literalism) to express a sense of urgent admonition for the temperate life:

> Had our first parents been less presumptuous, had they paused to count the cost of the rash step they were about to take, had they in that early morning of the race, and of their own existence, inquired into the deeper meanings and purpose of life, we their descendants, might have been spared at least, from experiencing the deeper meanings of sin. . . . In their transgression, unfortunately, they were to be the prototypes of millions who were to follow—millions in every age, millions in our age, thousands all about us, hundreds whom we know. Such persons are those who while blessed with youth, [made] the same "fatal mistake," reaching out after the things that are pleasing to the eye, gratifying to the senses, they bartered away a whole life of usefulness and happiness for one moment of sensuous enjoyment.[23]

It is to be expected that the presumed link between the world of eternal verities and the workaday world would not remain totally confined to the realm of purely philosophical speculation, but would be linked to the specific contours of the Christian faith itself insofar as that faith sought to meet the challenges of everyday life. It was never doubted that among the possible religious orientations of which African Americans could avail themselves, Christianity afforded the most viable ethic and the most plausible religion to effect a truly moral society.

In the words of Rev. E. W. D. Isaacs, corresponding secretary of the Baptist Young People's Union of the National Baptist Convention, "Christianity is the little leaven that leaveneth the whole lump of morality. Society cannot, yea, it will not travel long in the right path without the religion of Jesus Christ."[24] Roscoe Conkling Bruce, a noted columnist and writer of the period, saw a real functional link between the influence of the Christian faith and the weal of society insofar as temperate persons form society. Said Bruce in 1903 before the graduating class of the M Street High School of Washington, D.C.: "Religion and the church have, from a certain point of view, two main functions—first, to make peace between human society and assumed spiritual beings; and second, to antagonize anti-social acts and tendencies."[25]

A Focus on Christian Character

We have seen so far that black clergy and academics affirmed a realm of enduring principles that governs the "nature of things," a just moral universe superintended by God. A creative link exists between these two realms and awaits discovery by the disciplined and inspired mind. Such a discovery provides entrance into the life lived as a "constant delight," a temperate life lived before God. The weal of society is ensured by such living, undergirded by Christian faith. Such religion provides stability, integrity, and a sense of moral order.

But perhaps the capstone to the musing about the nature of the life of virtue was the idea of character, especially Christian character. The prominence of this aspect of virtue, first articulated in the 1830s, resurfaces at century's end by these new proponents of virtue. Conscious as they were of the self-imposed demands on the race as it sought the means for social progress and uplift, they focused on Christian character as a crucial building block in forming a life of virtue.

William H. Thomas, author of *The American Negro: What He Was, What He Is, and What He Is to Become,* asked, "What is the opportunity and duty of self-respecting Negro Christianity for religious awakening, for loyal agreement, for nobility of purpose, for life now and hereafter?" Thomas's answer suggested the essence of the virtuous life: "Its chief and foremost duty is to make character the sole test and criterion of a Christian life, and to see to it that life devoid of courage, veracity, sincerity, and honest piety is not rated as a Christian character."[26]

One of the most spectacular events in the lives of African Americans just after the turn of the new century was the Negro Young People's Christian and Educational Congress, held in Atlanta, August 6–11, 1902. At least two hundred national and local race leaders converged on Atlanta to discuss their place in U.S. society from four perspectives: religion, social and moral reform, material prosperity, and education. The idea of character repeatedly surfaced as a theme during the congress, especially as the problem of negotiating through the treacherous racial rapids of the United States was contemplated. Bishop W. J. Gaines, the president of the congress, set the tone for the meeting in his welcome address by affirming, "In the sharp contentions incident to the civilization in which the American Negro finds himself, he must be supported by intelligence and Christian character to keep abreast with his environment, and work out a high destiny for himself."[27]

Bishop Gaines might have been a bit too sanguine about the racial situation when he declared that "with intelligence and Christian character as his foundation, the Negro has nothing to fear. His troubles will take wings and fly away." But he felt that if the black man would "plant himself upon the everlasting principles of righteousness, the race problem would adjust itself naturally under such a condition, for God has ordained that a good and wise people will prosper anywhere and everywhere."

The acquisition of Christian character by African Americans was thus a tool that would presumably be useful in wresting equitable treatment from society. At the same time character was the result of creative appropriation of the rigors that racism had imposed upon them in society. It had been the product of fire.

H. T. Kealing, for years the editor of the *African Methodist Episcopal Review*, spoke eloquently at the congress of these rigors, and implicitly of the virtue of perseverance that helped explain how blacks could continue under such arduous circumstances. For Kealing, "the Negro, cast upon the barren shore of American slavery, has been able to feed upon the toil, the tears and contempt before which other men die, till he stands today a fruitful tree transmuting his very trials into food for Christian character and manly stamina."[28]

In an essay prepared for a volume edited by Booker T. Washington and W. E. B. DuBois called *The Negro Problem*, Kealing could offer an inspiring paean to the black person's indomitable spirit in the midst of hostility:

> The Negro's excellences have entered into American character and life already; so have his weaknesses. He has

brought cheer, love, emotion and religion in saving measure to the land. He has given it wealth by his brawn and
liberty by his blood. His self-respect, even in abasement,
has kept him struggling upward; his confidence in his own
future has infected his friends and kept him from nursing
despondency or planning anarchy.[29]

Albert A. Tennant, writing a piece titled "True Nobility" in the
Colored American Magazine, discerned a measure of perseverance
within black strivings as character was shaped and tested. He believed,
"The aim of truly great men is to mould character. With the rough
and scanty material at their command they toil incessantly. The arduous tasks teach courage and the humble surroundings sympathy—
these form an ideal character on which, alone, true nobility rests."[30]

The Value of a Good Home

Perhaps no generation of Americans at any time in the history of this
country could appreciate the home with as much reverence as did
the sons and daughters of slaves who came to full maturity during
the latter years of the nineteenth century. The home was for that
generation a distinct locus for stability and order, unlike the slave
quarters of bygone days, which could be violated at will by the master, an overseer, or any white man. There was a certain precariousness
in the slave home, though slaves managed to maintain a surprising
level of intact kinship systems. It is not an exaggeration to say that
for the generation of blacks at the end of the century, the home, free
from the threats of disintegration inherent in the slave system, took
on near sacrosanct proportions of meaning. Even a white southerner,
in reflecting on that period, could say with a great deal of sympathy
for this home: "It [the home] takes on a sanctity that extends to
every member of the family and decent living is the rule. No stranger
may at night signal in the shutters of this house, no woman venture
forth to roam the streets. It has become the home of self-respecting
American citizens."[31]

In fact, without the home one was not able to comprehend the
mysteries of successful personal nurturing, the flow of racial history,
or the process of which society is made integral and whole. William
A. Sinclair, in *The Aftermath of Slavery,* wrote, "To this appreciation
of the home and the recognition of its obligations may be ascribed

not only much of the prosperity, progress, and happiness which freedom has brought to the colored race, but it is also the rock on which
the race must build to insure its salvation and a glorious future."[32]

Sinclair went on to suggest that in the struggle upward,

> the colored people need only to continue along all lines
> and stand firmly for liberty; be faithful to the churches, pa-
> tronize the school, support the colored press, encourage
> professionals, *cultivate the home life,* practice thrift and
> economy, honor those North and South who champion
> the cause of freedom; and these shall be unto them the
> forces of the Lord of Hosts, which shall overturn the op-
> pressor and redeem a people.[33]

While Sinclair viewed the home as instrumental in providing a
foundation for positive social change, others viewed the home as a
source for social stability. The suggestion was made, at least on the
theoretical level, that good and stable government is related to the
nature of the homes of the nation.

Rev. G. L. B. Blackwell, general secretary of the A.M.E. Zion
Church, declared that "the foundation of all government rests in the
home of the citizens. . . . The embryonic seed of government gener-
ates, germinates and produces a state of government commensurate
with the predominant type of the homes represented. This is especially true in a republic." If, for Blackwell, the virtues inherent in
character—"high ideals of honor, . . . economy, justice and truth"—
are "emphasized and inculcated in the minds of the youth around
the hearthstone, lived out in the homes of the home makers, thus far
will the government of the state rise, and no higher." If, however,

> the majority of the citizens are ignorant and vicious then
> will the government be corrupt; then will the iron heel of
> an educated and bigoted minority—made so through the
> knowledge of superior environment and attainment—be
> set upon the necks of this ignorant mass, and then will
> ensue constant and bitter strife between these opposing el-
> ements, profligacy versus morality, ignorance versus en-
> lightenment, prodigality versus economy—and there is no
> question of the outcome.[34]

While the home clearly was a benefit to the wider society and the state, it was also viewed as the unique place in society where interpersonal skills and roles between persons and sexes were developed and played out.

Professor George L. Tyus of Washington, Arkansas, put forth a view of the link between the home and family and the significant roles that members of the household embodied: "By a well-established home we mean that sacred spot which constitutes the center of our affection, around which two hearts beat as one. The place which (as has been said) is the father's kingdom, the mother's world and the children's paradise; the place where all strife is shut out and a sea of love shut in."[35]

Professor Tyus's description of the home may appear by today's standard hopelessly sexist and condescending to women. In that respect perhaps most people of that time shared his view. Yet there is evidence that many African American proponents of virtue were able to interpret Christian faith, and the perceived roles of men and women in the home, in such a way that a real basis for complementarity between the sexes was possible.

St. George Richardson, president of Edward Waters College in Jacksonville, Florida, expressed a hope for "happy homes where father and mother are in accord both in spirit and body. There should be more regard paid to the spiritual injunction, 'Be ye not unequally yoked together.'"[36] Similarly, while Dr. R. M. Hall could unabashedly say that a "good deal of the responsibility to help build the character of the young devolves upon the mother," he could declare that "fathers are also responsible for the moral nurturing of the young."[37] Archdeacon James S. Russell of Lawrenceville, Virginia, urged that "the father or mother of every family should set up the family altar and officiate regularly thereat, that the young of the household may imbibe and put into practice the sacred lessons learned thereat."[38]

Rev. J. A. Whitted did not exempt men from an active role in the home in the nurturing of children, particularly sons. He said, "Christian fathers in the spirit of the Bible will necessarily produce men of the proper stamp," while "Christian mothers in alliance with other Christian mothers . . . will give to the world daughters whose crowns will be beautiful with chastity and virtue."[39]

Despite some suggestions that a degree of complementarity existed between the sexes, the impression is inescapable that African American men and women, and most Americans of that era, genuinely viewed the home as the "mother's world." They believed that within the family circle, men and women occupied two different but equally important spheres, though the two spheres existed in some degree of mutuality. Rosetta Douglass Sprague, the daughter of Frederick Douglass, believed that "the educated Negro woman will find that her greatest field for effective work is in the home."[40]

Miss Mary A. Lynch of Livingstone College in North Carolina stated,

> The strongest point in favor of woman's capacity is the manner in which she has filled her special sphere to which God has divinely called her, the home. The efficiency with which she has molded within its sacred walls the character of the statesmen who have legislated for the world, the clergymen who have evangelized the world, the educators who have taught the world, the professional men and women who have followed their respective callings and the women who have mothered the world. Women have been the civilizers of mankind.[41]

Yet even in a rather socially conservative age, it was not altogether unthinkable for black women to make their mark and living in the world outside the home. Such work was certainly conceivable and not to be discouraged, but the special role for women in shaping the environment of the home remained more critical.

In a very forceful address delivered before the Negro Young People's Congress entitled "A Pure Motherhood, the Basis of Racial Integrity," Mrs. Addie W. Hunton of Normal, Alabama, allowed that "we have seen in abundance the fruits of her devotion to the church. We have witnessed her as a leader in social and moral reforms. Her integrity and faithfulness in positions of honor and trust in the business world have been attained." But, added Mrs. Hunton, "It is in the uplifting and purifying of the home that her greatest work has been wrought, and there rests her greatest responsibility to God and the human race." The work of women had divine sanction in Mrs. Hunton's estimation, for "to woman is given the sacred and divine trust of developing the germ of life—it is her peculiar function to sustain, nourish, train, and educate the future man."[42]

The special and divine sanction conferred upon woman and mother meant that there devolved upon her an equally pronounced degree of responsibility. If "woman is the power behind the throne, then," asked Mrs. Mattie A. Ford of Atlanta, "what woman would not rise in all her power and strength God has given her to do her part to protect her home and its sacred surroundings from sin, vice and unhappiness?"[43] Mrs. I. Garland Penn, the young wife of one of the organizers of the congress, believed that "it is the mother's duty to so live and demean herself that the influence thrown around the children may be the purest and best, so that she may present to society, to the state and to God children with good morals and right conceptions of life and its purpose."[44]

The emphasis on responsibility and the woman's "doing her part" produced a unique model of demeanor and behavior for the African American woman of the late nineteenth and early twentieth centuries. A disdain for the frivolous, the cultivation of strength of character, and a willingness to sacrifice would mark such a woman. While not a participant at the 1902 Negro Young People's Christian and Educational Congress, Mrs. B. E. Bradford nevertheless reflected the point of view at that meeting in articles she wrote for a popular journal during the same decade. Mrs. Bradford described the ideal African American woman as one who was "garbed in quiet apparel, plain and simple in dress, gracious in manners, courteous to strangers, kind and self sacrificing to those whose lot is more trying. She may not be handsome, yet she is a woman that everyone is pleased to meet. Her expression is one of contentment, love and piety; people confide and trust in her, secure in the knowledge that their confidence will not be betrayed."

Juxtaposed to this model of woman was the "gaudily dressed human being, with form artificial, her face expressing the pride, arrogance and discontent." Yet "these creatures are not women, but counterfeit imitation beings whose lives are given to pleasure seeking, who find the first duties of home, husband and children too burdensome except perhaps when they desire to make a big display by giving mid-night suppers or a card party." Although these women may "have the face of Venus or the form of a Parisian model, they are far from being beautiful in the way that God intended them to be." Mrs. Bradford ended her paean to "Woman" by proudly saying that "we do not envy them their fair faces and perfect forms, or their fine feathers, except in proportion as they create envy and extravagance in good women, who would otherwise make good wives and useful women in the community in which they live."[45]

At the 1902 congress, women were asked to be vigilant lest forces outside the home destroy its sanctity, undermining the moral development of all within it. Mrs. I. Garland Penn entreated her audience "to build a strong wall of Godly defense around your homes, and have them well guarded by the ever-watchful eye of our Heavenly Father, who knows the trials and temptations that come to us." Above all things, she continued, "let us teach our boys to respect the virtue of all women, respecting them as they would have others respect their own sisters."[46]

But the same women, those who had attained some level of higher education, who were imbued with a sense of character and virtue, were asked to exert themselves on behalf of those of lesser ranking. Mrs. Mary Church Terrell, president of the National Association of Colored Women's Clubs, voiced this theme as she tirelessly went across the country organizing these clubs among black women. Stirred by their motto "Lifting As We Climb," they strove to touch the lives in positive ways of their lesser-appointed sisters. Mrs. Terrell said that as sisters of the same race, they would share the same destiny:

> Colored women of education and culture know that they cannot escape altogether the consequences of the acts of their most depraved sisters. They see that even if they were wicked enough to turn a deaf ear to the call of duty, both policy and self-preservation demand that they go down among the lawless, the illiterate and even the vicious, to whom they are bound by the ties of race and sex, and put forth every possible effort to reclaim them.[47]

Achieving Economic Independence

An interesting practical consequence of this emphasis on the sanctity of the home was the pronounced effort among African Americans of this generation to own a home rather than rent or lease someplace to live. Booker T. Washington, with his theme of economic preparedness for the race, declared before the 1902 congress that "one of the greatest curses of our race is the one-room cabin." Mary Church Terrell and her organization of Colored Women's Clubs were equally determined to end the economic and cultural dissipation exemplified by the one-room cabin.

Washington, who in slavery had been born in such a house, was referring to the ubiquitous little shack in the rural countryside of the South, which was rented by a black tenant farmer from a white landlord. Such a cabin was the symbol of economic dependency. It was quite consistent, therefore, that home ownership would be a cause espoused by people of this era who equally championed the ideals of character, strong manhood and womanhood, and the sanctity of the integral family around the honest hearth.

Harry Stillwell Edwards, a southern white who, like Washington, saw the value of developing a strong middle class among blacks as one means of solving racial tensions in the South, declared with almost naive forthrightness, "No man can expand to his full possibilities in a rented house. The Christian virtues blossom in their perfection about one's own fireside. Every lesson of morality, every elevated thought doubles its power and influence."[48] Black ownership of homes was for Edwards a means of entrance into the world of responsible citizenship and the securing of a stake in the public weal.

Although clearly sympathetic to the elevation of the Negro, Edwards was not without a sense of self-interest as an upholder of a stable society. He believed that if the Negro became a home owner, he would see "the force of arguments for low taxation, good streets, adequate police service, quick transportation. And seeing so much he eventually learns that his ballot must neither be suppressed or sold." Besides, "in protecting his own home, he would necessarily protect those of his white neighbors."

As a means of establishing effective lines of interest between blacks and the community, William H. Thomas advocated landownership. "Landownership is unquestionably," asserted Thomas, "a substantial factor in race improvement, . . . for the reason that a landowner, great or small, is a fixture in the community, and thereby acquires a vested right in its welfare and development."[49]

Mary Helm, a southern white, saw the economic and personal value that came with home ownership. "The increased sense of self-respect that comes from such an ownership [of a home] leads," thought Mrs. Helm, "to a deeper sense of obligation for the protection and maintenance of the home and the character of the family life. It also brings an increased sense of responsibility for the public good and of personal advantage in the preservation of law."[50]

During this period, a fairly pervasive view affirmed black economic independence as much as possible from the wider society and culture. This notion surfaced in the 1902 Negro Young People's Congress. Race progress would be measured to the extent that blacks could achieve a desired level of autonomy in running their own economic and cultural enterprises. Rev. W. Bishop Johnson, of the Educational Society of the National Baptist Convention, regarded the Educational Society and its program as working toward that level of independence: "It [the Educational Society] stands for the ownership, control and conduct of the institutions it supports. It promulgates the doctrine of manly self-help; the exhaustion of every effort of his [the Negro's] own in the support of the schools under its control, and the turning to other sources only as a last resort."[51]

Besides implying independence of an economic nature, race progress would be advanced to the extent that independent thinkers flourished within the race. W. S. Scarborough was of the opinion that "to assure the future of any people, there must be a growth in both thinking and doing. The Negro race must learn to think for itself, not to let others think for it; it must learn to do for itself along all lines, not be dependent upon others for such work."[52]

The African American home was understood as a place where national civic values could be nourished, and these proponents of virtue believed that a strong home would inculcate a particular love of African American race and culture as well. A well-ordered life in such a home was viewed as being quite consistent with the ultimate goal of race uplift and progress in the United States.

Mrs. Julia Mason Layton's advice to homemakers captured very aptly this vision of well-ordered domestic life and the inculcation of race pride:

> No matter how humble the home, how few articles, keep them whole and well polished and tastefully arranged. But of all, the most important, see to it, if there be but one piece of furniture, that it is paid for. Do not be a slave to

some installment house. Have a place for everything and everything in its place. From that day we start the home strive to start a good library—first, have a Bible; next, a dictionary. Then a history of the Negro race. Do not purchase the sentimental, trashy novels of to-day. Don't give them space at all. Let your purchases be of good, sound literature. Month by month add one good book; always endeavor to secure the books that have been written by our own people, that are good.[53]

Schooling as a Nurturer of Virtue

Besides the home, the school was perceived as a place wherein Christian character could be nurtured. Under the wise, firm, and compassionate tutelage of the competent teacher, the rough and unrefined young could be transformed into men and women who could offer meaningful service to their community and their people. Imbued as they were with a sense of urgency toward securing the integrity of the race, this generation viewed the school as a worthy supplement to the home in building strong and viable people.

Speaking before the Young People's Christian and Educational Congress of 1902, W. H. Lanier, president of a small normal college, was of the opinion that the "school must supplement the home," and because of that, an "awful responsibility accompanies the delightful opportunity for the teacher to render service by planting in the heart of the neglected child the seed of moral ideas and social acumen."[54]

In general, however, it was not presumed that the school should supplant the home in the process of character formation. As W. E. B. DuBois said, "They [the common and secondary schools] cannot and ought not to replace the home as the chief moral teacher."[55] Nevertheless, because the school and the teacher had such obvious potential for exerting influence in the African American community and for securing for that community a modicum of equitable treatment in society, it is just that we treat the school and the teacher in the same fashion as the home was treated as a harbinger for the inculcation of virtue and character.

Of singular importance in the development of African American education was the role of religious bodies and denominations. In addition to the A.M.E. Church and the A.M.E. Zion Church, which were notable in their educational thrusts before the Civil War, many of the denominations planted colleges and normal schools for black people who were freed after the Civil War. Almost invariably, the educational policy of the schools was a judicious blend of piety and pedagogy.

W. H. Crogman unabashedly proclaimed that "these schools are Christian schools." Rev. Henry L. Morehouse, after whom Morehouse College was named, averred that the "ruling idea in this educational work has been the formation of strong, intelligent Christian character; education dominated by a positive Christian spirit."[56] Rev. W. H. Weaver, a field secretary of the Board of Missions for Freedmen of the Presbyterian Church, described the work of his board thus: "This Board recognized and acts upon the principle and the fact that the greatest work it can do for the race is to help bring the individuals under the impress of the Christian life and character, under the sway of His personality, who was both the son of man and the son of God. For it was only as men are brought into this relation that their lives are bettered, sweetened and purified."[57]

Two very important ideas emerge as we assess the perceived role of the school in African American life and its ability to inculcate a sense of virtue. First, there are the role and character of the teacher and, second, the role of educational systems in the matter of race progress.

Turn-of-the-century proponents of virtue almost universally considered access to the world of the enlightened mind a critical factor without which no race progress would take place. And it is no surprise that the one figure without which the race could make progress was the teacher. Some people regarded teachers, strong of character and competency, in almost transcendent terms. Miss Charlotte E. Hawkins of Boston declared before members of the Negro Young People's Christian and Educational Congress that "these teachers, patient, loving, whose lives are instruments of God's hands, are they, upon whom depends the destiny of the Negro race."[58]

Rev. W. H. Weaver recognized that besides the content of the school curriculum, the role and character of the teacher were crucial in the educational process. "In the educational work of the board strict and careful attention is given not only to the character of the instruction, but also," asserted Weaver, "to the character and qualifications of the instructors." For Weaver, "the aim [was to secure] the best teachers, possessing that mental power which assures certainty in discernment, clearness in explanation, and who are in character and demeanor such as will influence in the right way and inspire to right doing and living." The litmus test for the teachers' success was "seen in the manners and morals of their pupils and in the earnest Christian work and sustained Christian lives of graduates."[59]

The character and demeanor of the teacher were pronounced issues because of the perceived needs of the child. Rev. G. Edward Read, the president of Spiller Academy in Hampton, Virginia, viewed the child as the "central figure in all educational systems." The child's "powers are multiplex, his possibilities well nigh infinite." Read believed that "the former may be unfolded in their natural order by the skillful teacher, while the latter he may only direct by inspiring to lofty endeavor."[60] Read was fascinated by the infinite possibilities of early childhood. Indeed one may detect in him such an appreciation of the mystery attendant to the young life that a view of almost religious proportions emerges. Listen to his description of the relationship between the teacher and such a life yet to be fashioned: "He [the teacher] is not dealing with material things; he is assisting in the development of an immortal idea. Hand in hand with the intellectual training should proceed that moral life, that character building with which the teacher is the molder, builder and architect of his school. As his conception of education grows and expands, so will his workmanship become more perfect and symmetrical."

It is then no wonder that, in the words of Rev. D. G. Mill of Washington, D.C., "the teacher should guard his own life well." Why? Because for Mill, "the first ten or twelve years of life the character of the child is principally formed by imitation and example."[61] Just as character grew best in the soil of the truly pious and Christian home, so did personal worth and character of the teacher develop within the riches of the Christian faith.

Professor W. S. Scarborough, a respected scholar of his day, was unequivocal in this regard: teachers "must be religious, God-fearing, Christian men and women." Moreover, asserted Scarborough, "the Bible must be their standard and religion a part of their lives. Not the frothy kind that has only a religious vocabulary without a religious experience, but the kind that can stand the fiercest light."[62]

Because of the peculiar pedagogical and moral needs posed by the child whose possibilities for development were infinite, an awesome responsibility devolved upon the teacher. Only those whose character and moral stature were as great as the needs brought to them could be considered worthy teachers. Scarborough was of the opinion that the "teacher, like the preacher, stands too near the young to be other than thoroughly honorable." He further believed, "Weak, unprincipled, selfish persons with no race pride, no race love, no race hope, should not be found at the teacher's desk. Those who teach must be men and women in whom frivolity finds no lodgment, who are not only above reproach, but who possess such force of character that they can implant in our young strength of discrimination between right and wrong and resolution to follow light and do the right."[63]

Besides the obvious value of the character-filled teacher for the pupil, the teacher had worth for the weal of the society as a whole. Professor J. W. Gilbert declared boldly, "No class of workers contribute more to the stability of the government and to domestic tranquility than the true teacher. The teacher it is who ought to give the earliest moral discipline that prepares the community for higher and broader views of duty in all the multifarious details of the intricate relations of community life."[64]

Because the teacher acts to sensitize students and others to the moral texture that obtains in the truly good society, the teacher is one of the clearest embodiments of what many African American thinkers of this era called civic righteousness. Professor Ernest L. Chew, the principal of a public school in Atlanta, spoke in a very eloquent and moving manner of this civic righteousness:

> The public school teacher is the prophet, priest and warrior of civic righteousness. Through prayer and meditation he has evolved an ideal of State, where the environment will conduce to symmetrical development of character in all; irrespective of adventitious circumstances; where the possibilities of each nature may be realized; where wayward youth will be recalled to paths of rectitude and usefulness; where wealthy offender and petty criminal shall work in chains together; where honest toil brings just recompense, where politics is an incidental experience of all and the

profession of none. Such is the schoolmaster's phantom city, such the school teacher's New Jerusalem, which he prophesies and would help us bring down from above.[65]

Such a lofty vision of the good society could, in the view of President Inman E. Page of Langston University in Oklahoma, find a foundation in outlines of the U.S. constitutional experience. Page observed that "because the founders of the American republic made provision for the establishment of schools to be under the control of the government they emphasized the relation which they expected the teacher to sustain to all matters of a civil and political character."[66]

There is no doubt that Page appreciated the essentially conservative function of this relation, for "the teacher in an American school should take the child who is placed in his charge and give him such training as will prepare him to be a useful citizen." Page's view, however, does not necessarily lead to uncritical conformity on the part of the child, for a part of the "usefulness" of citizenship learned in the relation with the teacher is the acquisition of the sense of "right—as God has given him to see the right." Seeking the right, inculcating a measure of virtue within students so that they could seek to live within a truly inclusive national community, was seen within the scope of the teacher's work. Page concluded his unique view of the teacher's role in the national purpose by saying:

> Our political system makes it imperative that civic righteousness shall be the theme of every teacher from the kindergarten to the university. . . . For when the teacher is giving this instruction he is teaching his pupils that as citizens they must not only have virtue but they must deal justly and fairly with their fellow-citizens, be they white or black, rich or poor; that in their relations to one another in matters pertaining to the government they must know no race, no color, or class or creed, or section; and that unless this course is pursued there can be no national prosperity, no national purpose.[67]

Typically Bourgeois?

It should be apparent that the people who came to prominence in the first and second generations after the end of chattel slavery in this country were a distinct set of men and women indeed. Using our terminology of today, they would probably be termed solid members of the middle class or the black bourgeoisie. Yet because of the connotations that have come to be associated with the terms—cultural vapidness, an uncritical acceptance of the status quo, a paucity of independent thinking—such terms when applied to this generation would be unfortunate and would not do them justice. Solid they were; worshipers of class they were not.

If they upheld values that today are denounced as hopelessly bourgeois, they acted because espousal of such values was deemed useful for the progress of a race not yet forty years removed from chattel slavery. They had their standards—standards that were very much antithetical to the diminished standards of behavior and self-worth to which racist slaveholders had attempted to subject their fathers and mothers. Furthermore, a new world in a new century was dawning, and urgency was the watchword.

On the night of August 11, 1902, Bishop W. J. Gaines mounted the podium to bid farewell to the two hundred or so delegates to the Negro Young People's Christian and Educational Congress. The redoubtable old divine, a fixture in the African Methodist Episcopal Church, sent them on their way with these words: "This Congress has made clear the fact that the Negro realizes that after all it is his own worth and value as a man and as a citizen that are to determine his position and his place in this country."[68]

The men and women who heard these words were persuaded that through a creative appropriation of Christian faith in the context of history and society and through the development of sound Christian character, their sense of virtue would produce a generation of worth to their race, to their God, and to their descendants.

Conclusion

MY MAIN CONCERN in this book has been to document as carefully and widely as possible historic remnants and depositories of virtue within the social consciousness of African Americans, and to understand how the quest for virtue functioned in the struggle for freedom, personal and corporate identity, and racial uplift among African Americans. Let me summarize before drawing out implications for the present.

Employing Virtue to Develop Self and Castigate Injustice

We have seen in this study how an often beleaguered and oppressed community came to understand and interpret an ethical ideal—the pursuit of virtue—in ways that were consistent with, indeed supportive of, their strivings for freedom and social integrity. The four virtues—prudence, justice, perseverance, and temperance—were all understood, interpreted, and refashioned to mitigate the personal and corporate suffering, the economic and political marginalization, and attempts by the wider society to dehumanize black people.

We have defined African American virtue as a vision of an ordered life in which the disciplined intellect enables persons to struggle against injustice and to forge communities and lifestyles that could ensure the development of the furthest moral and material possibilities of African Americans. We have seen how the pursuit of virtue, and the cultivation of the four cardinal virtues, that is to say, prudence, justice, perseverance, and temperance, have been articulated and understood throughout African American social history. Throughout that history, in slavery and in freedom, virtue functioned as an idea that gave shape and focus to aspirations to African American integrity. The cultivation of virtue has provided the basis for the development of a distinct social consciousness within the historical experience of African Americans. This consciousness has been forged in the crucible of the bitter experiences of slavery and further deepened in the political and social constraints imposed upon black people even during the years of freedom.

We are now many years removed from those generations of African Americans who first articulated the need for the pursuit of virtue and its importance in the struggle for dignity, freedom, justice from the state, and the full embodiment of character for themselves. Early proponents of African American virtue, such as Maria Stewart, James Forten Sr., and Hosea Easton, articulated a call for freedom from slavery and a call for racial integrity and couched such calls within the idea of virtue. Later on, in the aftermath of the terrible enslavement that had plagued their mothers, fathers, and forebears, subsequent generations sought to build their lives and secure firm foundations for their families. Poised as they were on the edge of a new century, they pondered and agonized over the future of the race, especially as that race faced the particularly virulent forms of racism during the post-Reconstruction period after the Civil War. These generations appropriated the tradition of virtue formation within the context of the continued struggle for justice and race uplift and shaped it to meet their challenges.

At the conclusion of such a study, one must seek to discern its relevance to the critical questions facing African Americans today, poised now on the eve of yet a new century. I devote the last pages of this work to a consideration of these issues. But before addressing the issues raised by such a concern, we do well to reiterate some of the salient points in the visions of virtue that this study has revealed.

The focus on virtue is concerned with the integrity of the *being* and *person* of the moral actor. Insistence on the primacy of inner being is critical. On a theoretical level it has been argued that African American proponents of virtue were so imbued with such a concept because they were intent on rebutting the implicit racist suggestion that the inner being of blacks or slaves was of no account, that at best it was an entity that did not warrant serious attention. These African American proponents of virtue were perhaps among the first of their color and of a philosophical lineage that cried out, "I am of worth! You will not enslave or dehumanize me!"

With the affirmation of their being and its inherent integrity came the self-imposed responsibility to embody aspects of excellence of character, to be just, mentally disciplined, persevering, and temperate. In short, demands for a just world assumed self-imposed demands for the pursuit of virtue. We must never lose sight of the fact that the earliest proponents of virtue among African Americans and their later successors were always imbued with a critical consciousness, that is to say, a desire to critique the society that ostracized them and the government that countenanced such oppression. A call to virtue would entail demanding that the United States be a just and virtuous state, free from the moral scourge of slavery and racial discrimination and, at the same time, an African American community characterized by just and temperate living. Critical consciousness was thus directed outwardly and inwardly.

I would propose that the vision of virtue is still being forged to the extent that the dual-faceted critical consciousness is still evident among African Americans. We might expect to find vestigial elements of the historic social consciousness that virtue undergirded in the past wherever there is a nexus of a critical consciousness directed at inequities in our society and a corresponding desire among African Americans to nurture personal rectitude and the pursuit of virtue. The quest for virtue was born in the actual struggle of black people to define themselves in human and virtuous terms when the culture around them was demeaning their humanity. Claiming virtue was their way of insisting on their humanity and their desire to lead lives as free, self-possessing men and women.

Virtues in the Current Context

We have postulated that the four cardinal virtues helped shape the contours of African American aspirations to full humanity and provided a measure of social integrity and uplift for the race. To what extent, one might ask, are these four cardinal virtues, and indeed the idea of virtue itself, relevant, apparent, or available to us today as we contemplate the social environment in which African Americans now find themselves? Perhaps the most critical aspects of the historic definition of virtue that bear continuing scrutiny within the contemporary context are prudence and the focus on the disciplined intellect, justice and the quest for structures that can ensure the furthest material possibilities for African Americans, the virtue of fortitude and an ethos of sustained effort, and temperance and the vision of an ordered life. We turn now to discuss each of these aspects of virtue in African American life.

In 1976, Jesse Jackson, always the indefatigable warrior for social justice, seemed to take a pause from his quite necessary and justifiable attacks on the power structure that had too long denied black ascendancy to focus on issues over which black people presumably had considerable control: the values that animated their existence and consciousness. In an article entitled "Give the People a Vision," Jackson decried the general ethical collapse that had plagued inner cities characterized by predatory criminal activity, self-destructive drug abuse, and community disintegration. He affirmed that the time was right to try some new approaches in the quest for social betterment and that among those new approaches would be those based on "new values." The thrust of Jackson's argument was that "black Americans must begin to accept a larger share of responsibility for their lives."[1]

Almost reminiscent of the disciplined life Maria Stewart called for a century and a half earlier, Jackson called for soldiers in the battle against racism "who are strong, healthy, spirited, committed, well-trained and confident." Perhaps preoccupied by his presidential campaigns in the next decade, Jackson did not go on to develop more in depth and in a systematic way his conception of the role of these "new values" in the continuing struggle against racism and the fostering of the enterprise of black uplift. One suspects that had he done so, his thinking would have been surprisingly similar to the visions of early African American proponents of virtue, which this study has identified.

That not done, it was left to commentators much more to the right than Jackson, actually so-called neoconservatives, who could embrace the notion of virtue, supported to be sure by white conservatives, thereby shrouding an idea that had historically been the impetus for radical social change in reactionary garb. That was unfortunate. Black America missed an opportunity to avail itself of a tradition that had provided so much spiritual and intellectual ballast in times that were surely more dire than the times in which we are now living.

The time is still ripe for a public dialogue on the role of virtue in African American public and private life and the extent to which the virtues can become the basis for a truly liberated existence for African Americans. Although it is difficult to encompass all of the aspects of that discussion, let me hasten to suggest some broad outlines of that enterprise.

The earliest proponents of an African American vision of virtue were embattled against cultural forces and a pervasive ideology that presumed black intellectual and moral inferiority. Such ideas were used to justify the enslavement of Africans and the assignment of freed blacks to a second-class status. The early proponents were determined that their minds would not be shackled, despite the undue constraints placed on their aspirations to full political and civil status as citizens. They earnestly believed that the route to power was through knowledge, and they were determined to develop contexts in which such knowledge could be attained, the intellect developed and nourished. The first reading rooms, literary associations, and schools for children were attempts to embody the pursuit of this virtue.

To be sure, consistent with its classical understanding, prudence was in the minds of African American proponents of virtue always applied intellect, or enlightenment that is able to effect discernible consequences in the world. We would expect to find such intellect when a critical consciousness is brought to bear on issues that have the potential for either improving or eroding the quality of people's lives.

One observation that remains indelibly etched in my mind at the conclusion of this study is the role of the public intellectual and the public nature of ethical discourse. African American social consciousness has been nurtured by and challenged by public intellectuals who were totally engaged in the struggle of their people.

But in a sense, the men and women who applied their critical consciousness to the issues of their time were not intellectuals in the specialized sense that we understand that term today, that is to say, persons who make their living primarily by the reflection on and promulgation of ideas. With earlier African American proponents of virtue, it may be said that a sense of vocation characterized a melding of private sensibilities and public exertions into a seamless garment. The firebrand pamphleteer David Walker ran a shop near the waterfront in Boston; Maria Stewart thought of herself primarily as a teacher; James Forten Jr. inherited and ran his father's sail-making business. All managed to bridge a gap between the purely private and the purely public to such an extent that agitation for social change was the result.

A confluence also exists between the calls for retributive justice from the American social system on the one hand, and the sobering challenges that devolve upon black people as distributive justice is worked out in that social system. The demands for retributive justice from the American social structures will, and should, continue to focus on the extent to which the American social system denies the full inclusion of black people in that system. Distributive justice, however, with its concern for the reciprocity that exists between citizens in a just society, considers as well the *responsibilities* each person has toward others within that social system. Discrimination upheld by law or legal structures must be consistently challenged and struck down. Yet the goal and essence of distributive justice would suggest heightened attention to the issue of the relations among members of the body politic. Moreover, at some point in time, a heightened and sophisticated awareness of the implications of distributive justice could be of profound importance in the ways African Americans continue to exercise their rights and responsibilities as citizens, critical of legal structures that deny justice but responsible to structures that ostensibly ensure justice.

African American proponents of virtue have also been exemplars of those having the virtue of fortitude or perseverance. This has been a necessary, constituent aspect of virtue itself. The ability to sustain a consistent effort in the struggle for justice despite great obstacles is due in part to the clarity of the vision for justice that an enlightened intellect is able to discern. Spiritual vitality is necessary to develop and maintain a sufficient level of fortitude and perseverance. Black people have always had to depend upon their ability to endure the onslaughts of outrageous fortune during their sojourn within hostile social environments. Perseverance must always be in great supply for the outnumbered, those temporarily overpowered.

The lesson from our study of historic visions of virtue would suggest that perseverance must have purpose, must always be linked to a vision of a good that justifies and undergirds the tenacity summoned to adequately endure the hardship of the moment. What is suggested here is a fresh reenvisioning of the problem of black suffering, pain, and anxiety in such a way that human hope is reconciled with human purposeful exertion in the midst of suffering. Robert Gordon's quirky but insightful imagery of the "steam engine of a race" is still evocative of a search for an enduring vision that can undergird the virtue of perseverance.

Finally, in an age in which elements of the general American psyche seem to be captured by unbridled materialism, sensuality, and dysfunctional behavior, temperance would seem to be a particularly important virtue, but it is no more critical or less important than any of the other cardinal virtues; the excellence of a person's character is hinged on all four. Nevertheless, temperance strikes us as particularly important when we consider the enormous social costs associated with dysfunctional and intemperate lifestyles. To be sure, the despair that discrimination can cause can take its toll on the human spirit and surely plays a role in the high levels of substance abuse within the African American community. And to some extent, one wonders if reckless sexual behavior might not have its genesis in the throes of misshapen personalities that grow all too often and tragically in the soil of societal indifference to human problems.

It makes no sense to blame the victim in matters of spiritual impairment. And yet, we must remember that virtue theory, and particularly insights relative to the virtue of temperance, suggests that intemperate behavior proceeds from some internal chaotic core, a lack of a vision of an ordered existence that could mitigate the warring urges within the self. As a virtue, temperance has helped to shape the African American response to attempts to impose social chaos upon that community. Temperance connotes the concept of an ordered and disciplined life. Temperance not only includes an aversion against certain debilitating and self-destructive practices, but it also includes a full acceptance and embrace of a total lifestyle characterized by order, moderation, and balance. The recovery of temperance for African Americans in our contemporary times would certainly pay close attention to practices that tend to erode a sense of ordered space, moral autonomy, and balance.

The vision of an African American sense of virtue that informs social consciousness directs the disciplined intellect to ensure that the structures of U.S. society are so constructed that the furthest material possibilities of African Americans can be effected. Besides the obvious allusion to economic well-being suggested by the term, material possibilities can include access to political structures of power as well, since in reality the course of economic affairs is determined by policy decisions made within the political domain. At the same time, an accent on virtue would require that some attention be paid to issues of personal responsibility within the civic domain, requirements for personal rectitude and responsible behavior. But above all, the legacy of virtue as an idea that has informed African American critical social consciousness is the ability to overcome the narrow vision of one person's will to dehumanize another human being and the ultimate triumph of the human spirit.

Notes

Preface

1. Maria Stewart, *The Productions of Mrs. Maria W. Stewart* (Boston: Friends of Freedom and Virtue, 1835), 61.

2. Henry Highland Garnet, "The Past and the Present Condition and the Destiny of the Colored Race," in *Negro Social and Political Thought, 1850–1920,* ed. Howard Brotz (New York: Basic Books, 1966), 201.

3. For a fine exposition of how virtue and particular virtues are viewed as constituent of African and African American social consciousness I am indebted to a recent work by Peter J. Paris, *The Spirituality of African Peoples: The Search for a Common Moral Discourse* (Minneapolis: Fortress Press, 1995). My concern is to document the *historical grounding* of virtue in African American social consciousness, while Paris is concerned to show enduring social manifestations in a cross-cultural analysis of peoples of African descent.

1. Virtue and African American Existence

1. Louis Hughes, *Thirty Years a Slave: From Bondage to Freedom* (Milwaukee: South Side Press, 1897), 79.

2. A Free Negro, "Slavery," in *Negro Orators and Their Orations,* ed. Carter G. Woodson (New York: Russell and Russell, 1925), 25.

3. Ibid., 28.

4. Josef Pieper, *The Four Cardinal Virtues* (Notre Dame, Ind.: University of Notre Dame Press, 1966), xii.

5. T. H. Breen and Stephen Innes, *"Myne Owne Ground": Race and Freedom on Virginia's Eastern Shore* (New York: Oxford University Press, 1980), 68.

6. *The Liberties of the Massachusetts Colony in New England,* in *Civil Rights and the Black American,* ed. Albert P. Blaustein and Robert L. Zangrando (New York: Simon & Schuster, 1968), 8; italics added.

7. Henry Bibb, *Narrative of the Life and Adventures of Henry Bibb, an American Slave* (1850; reprint, New York: Negro Universities Press, 1969), 18.

8. Austin Steward, *Twenty-two Years a Slave and Forty Years a Freeman* (1856; reprint, New York: Negro Universities Press, 1969), 327.

9. Ibid.

10. Frederick Douglass, "The Nature of Slavery," in *Negro Social and Political Thought*, 217.

11. J. W. C. Pennington, *The Fugitive Blacksmith: of Events in the History of James W. C. Pennington, Pastor of a Presbyterian Church, New York, formerly a slave in the State of Maryland, United States* (London: N.p., 1849), 15.

12. Steward, *Twenty-two Years a Slave*, 49.

13. Sidney W. Mintz and Richard Price, *An Anthropological Approach to the Afro-American Past: A Caribbean Perspective* (Philadelphia: Institute for the Study of Human Issues, 1976), 35.

14. A Free Negro, "Slavery," 28.

15. Ibid.

16. Sterling Stuckey, "Through the Prism of Folklore," *Massachusetts Review* 9 (1968): 417–37. See also the Introduction in Stuckey's *Slave Culture: Nationalist Theory and the Foundations of Black America* (New York: Oxford University Press, 1987).

17. Leon F. Litwack, *North of Slavery* (Chicago: University of Chicago Press, 1961), 3.

18. Martin Delaney, *The Condition, Elevation, Emigration, and Destiny of the Colored People of the United States* (1852; reprint, New York: Arno Press and New York Times, 1969), 14.

19. "Memorial of the Free People of Colour in Baltimore," *African Repository*, December 1826.

20. Maria W. Stewart, "Address Delivered at the Masonic Hall, Feb. 27, 1833," in *Productions of Mrs. Maria W. Stewart*, 64.

21. Rev. Amos Gerry Beman, "The Education of the Colored People," *Anglo-African Magazine* 1, no. 11 (November 1859): 338.

22. Pieper, *The Four Cardinal Virtues*, 146.

23. Frederick Douglass, "An Address to the Colored People of the United States," in *Negro Social and Political Thought*, 211–12.

2. The First Stirrings

1. Cotton Mather, *Diary of Cotton Mather*, vol. 1, 1681–1709 (New York: Frederick Ungar Publishing Co., 1911), 177. See also Lorenzo J. Greene, *The Negro in Colonial New England, 1620–1776* (New York: Columbia University Press, 1942), 266.

2. George Washington, *Writings*, ed. John C. Fitzpatrick (Washington, D.C.: N.p., 1931–44), 3:292; quoted in Edmund S. Morgan, *American Slavery . . . American Freedom: The Ordeal of Colonial Virginia* (New York: Norton, 1975), 4.

3. Celeste Michelle Condit and John Louis Lucaites, *Crafting Equality: America's Anglo-African Word* (Chicago: University of Chicago Press, 1993), 4.

4. A Lover of Constitutional Liberty, *The Appendix: or, some Observations on the expediency of the Petition of the Africans, living in Boston, etc., lately presented to the General Assembly of the Province. To which is annexed, the Petition referred to. Likewise, Thoughts of Slavery with a useful extract from the Massachu-*

setts Spy, of January 28,1773 by way of an Address to the Members of the Assembly, in *A Documentary History of the Negro People in the United States,* vol. 1, ed. Herbert Aptheker (New York: Citadel Press, 1951), 6–7.

5. *Petition to the Honbl. General Assembly of the State of Connecticut to be held at Hartford on the Second Thursday of Instant May, 1779—The Petition of the Negroes in the Towns of Stratford and Fairfield in the County of Fairfield who are held in a state of slavery,* in *A Documentary History of the Negro People,* 1:10.

6. Sidney Kaplan, *The Black Presence in the Era of the American Revolution, 1770–1800* (Washington, D.C.: Smithsonian Institution, 1973), 27.

7. Quoted in Roger Bruns, ed., *Am I Not a Man and a Brother: The Antislavery Crusade of Revolutionary America, 1688–1788* (New York: Chelsea House Publishers, 1977), 306.

8. Phillis Wheatley to Rev. Samson Occum, February 11, 1774, in *Am I Not a Man and a Brother,* 338.

9. Caesar Sarter, "Essay on Slavery," in *Am I Not a Man and a Brother,* 338.

10. Helen MacLam, "Black Puritan on the Northern Frontier: The Vermont Ministry of Lemuel Haynes," in *Black Apostles at Home and Abroad: The Black Christian Mission from the Revolution to Reconstruction,* ed. David Wills and Richard Newman (Boston: G. K. Hall, 1982), 5–6.

11. Vernon Loggins, *The Negro Author: His Development in America* (New York: Columbia University Press, 1931), 126.

12. Ruth Bogin, "Notes and Documents, 'Liberty Further Extended': A 1776 Antislavery Manuscript by Lemuel Haynes," *William and Mary Quarterly* 40 (January 1983): 85–105.

13. Lemuel Haynes, *The Nature and Importance of True Republicanism* (Rutland, Vt.: N.p., 1801), 11–12.

14. *Petition to His Excellency Thomas Gage, Esq., Captain General and Governor in Chief in and over this Province,* in *A Documentary History of the Negro People,* 9.

15. A Free Negro, "Slavery," 25.

16. *The Life and Confession of Johnson Green who is to be executed this day, August 17, 1786 for the Atrocious Crime of Burglary; together with his Last and Dying Words,* in *Early Negro Writing, 1760–1837,* ed. Dorothy Porter (Boston: Beacon Press, 1971), 405.

17. Greene, *The Negro in Colonial New England,* 152.

18. Richard Slotkin, "Narratives of Negro Crime in New England, 1675–1800," *American Quarterly* 25 (March 1973): 16.

19. Frances Smith Foster, *Witnessing Slavery: The Development of Ante-Bellum Slave Narratives* (Westport, Conn.: Greenwood Press, 1979), 39.

20. Kaplan, *The Black Presence,* 181.

21. August Meier and Elliot Rudwick, *From Plantation to Ghetto,* 3d ed. (New York: Hill and Wang, 1976), 99.

22. Kaplan, *The Black Presence,* 82.

23. Richard Allen, *The Life Experience and Gospel Labors of the Rt. Rev. Richard Allen* (Philadelphia: Martin and Boston, 1833).

24. *Constitution of the New York African Clarkson Association, New York, 1825*, in *Early Negro Writing*, 45–50.

25. *Laws of the African Society, instituted at Boston, 1796*, in *Early Negro Writing*, 9–12.

26. Prince Saunders, "An Address Delivered at Bethel Church, on the 30th of September 1818, before the Pennsylvania Augustine Society, for the Education of the People of Colour, To Which Is Annexed the Constitution of the Society," in *Early Negro Writing*, 90.

27. *Constitution of the Afric-American Female Intelligence Society of Boston*, in *Black Women in White America*, ed. Gerda Lerner (New York: Pantheon Books, 1972), 438.

28. *Laws of the African Society, instituted at Boston, 1796*, in *Early Negro Writing*, 11.

29. William Hamilton, "An Address to the New York African Society for Mutual Relief, Delivered in the Universalist Church, January 2, 1809," in *Early Negro Writing*, 37.

30. Prince Hall, "Pray God Give Us Strength to Bear Up under All Our Troubles," Masonic sermon delivered June 24, 1797, Menotomy, Massachusetts, Schomburg Center for Research in Afro-American Culture.

31. Peter Williams, "An Oration on the Abolition of the Slave Trade, Delivered in the African Church in the City of New York, January 1, 1808," in *Early Negro Writing*, 353.

32. Absalom Jones, "A Thanksgiving Sermon Preached January 1, 1808 on account of the Abolition of the African Slave Trade," in *Early Negro Writing*, 337.

33. Russell Parrott, "An Oration on the Abolition of the Slave Trade. Delivered on the First of January, 1814, at the African Church of St. Thomas, Philadelphia," in *Early Negro Writing*, 389.

34. Joseph Sidney, "An Oration Commemorative of the Abolition of the Slave Trade in the United States; delivered before the Wilberforce Philanthropic Association, in the City of New York, on the Second of January, 1809," in *Early Negro Writing*, 357.

35. Paul Dean, "A Discourse Delivered before the African Society of Boston on the Celebration of the Abolition of the Slave Trade," July 14, 1819, Schomburg Center for Research in Afro-American Culture.

36. Nathaniel Paul, "An Address Delivered on the Celebration of the Abolition of Slavery, in the State of New York, July 5, 1827," in *Negro Protest Pamphlets*, 18.

37. George Lawrence, "An Oration on the Abolition of the Slave Trade Delivered on January 1, 1813, in the African Methodist Episcopal Church," in *Early Negro Writing*, 375; italics added.

38. Ibid., 379.

39. Ibid.

3. African American Struggle and the Forging of Four Virtues

1. See especially Winthrop Jordan, *White over Black: American Attitudes toward the Negro, 1550–1812* (Chapel Hill: University of North Carolina Press, 1968), chaps. 11 and 15, and George M. Fredrickson, *The Black Image in the White Mind: The Debate on Afro-American Character and Destiny, 1817–1914* (New York: Harper & Row, 1971), chap. 1.

2. John Macquarie, *Dictionary of Christian Ethics* (Philadelphia: Westminster, 1967), 280.

3. Lawrence C. Becker and Charlotte B. Becker, *Encyclopedia of Ethics,* vol. 3 (New York: Garland Publishing, 1992), 1031.

4. Henry Highland Garnet, ed., *Walker's Appeal in Four Articles* (1848; reprint, New York: Arno Press and New York Times, 1969), v.

5. *Genius of Universal Emancipation* 11, no. 15 (April 1830), quoted in Loggins, *The Negro Author,* 86.

6. *Walker's Appeal,* vi.

7. David Walker, "Our Wretchedness in Consequence of Ignorance," in *Walker's Appeal,* 40, 42.

8. Ibid., 44.

9. Maria W. Stewart, "Religion and the Pure Principles of Morality, the Sure Foundation on Which We Must Build," in *The Productions of Mrs. Maria W. Stewart,* 4.

10. Stewart, "Address Delivered at the Masonic Hall," 64.

11. Rev. Joseph M. Corr, "Address Delivered before the Humane Mechanics, on the 4th of July, 1834," in *Early Negro Writing,* 147.

12. Ibid., 149.

13. "Address to the Free People of Colour of these United States, September 20, 1830," in *Proceedings of the Convention of Free Persons of Colour* (Philadelphia: N.p., 1831), reprinted in *Minutes and Proceedings of the National Negro Conventions, 1830–1864,* ed. Howard H. Bell (New York: Arno Press and New York Times, 1969), 11.

14. Editorial, "Education for Negroes," *Colored American,* March 4, 1837, 80.

15. *Minutes and Proceedings of the Convention of People of Colour, June 6–11, 1831* (1831; reprint, New York: Arno Press and New York Times, 1969), 5.

16. *Conventional Address of the Second Annual Convention of Free People of Color* (1832; reprint, New York: Arno Press and New York Times, 1969), 34.

17. Ibid.

18. Rev. J. W. C. Pennington, "The Self-Redeeming Power of the Colored Races of the World," *Anglo-African Magazine* 1, no. 10 (October 1859): 314.

19. Lawrence, "An Oration on the Abolition of the Slave Trade."

20. Steward, *Twenty-two Years a Slave,* 339.

21. Dorothy B. Porter, "The Organized Educational Activities of Negro Literary Societies," *Journal of Negro Education* 5 (October 1936): 560.

22. *Minutes and Proceedings of the Convention of People of Colour,* June 6–11, 1831, 6.

23. Beman, "The Education of the Colored People," 338.

24. *Colored American,* June 20, 1838.

25. Enid V. Barnett, "Education for Negroes in New York State, 1800–1860" (master's thesis, New York University, 1954), 63.

26. Lasalle Best, "An Account of Reading Rooms Established by Negroes in New York City," Federal Writers' Program Document, Schomburg Collection, New York Public Library.

27. Porter, "The Organized Educational Activities of Negro Literary Societies," 555–76.

4. The Quest for Justice and the Just State

1. Garnet, ed., *Walker's Appeal,* 16.

2. Stewart, *The Productions of Mrs. Maria W. Stewart,* 68.

3. The theodicy in Stewart's thought anticipates the views of Henry McNeil Turner a half century later. Both attempted to put the suffering of Africa and African Americans in a theological perspective by postulating the disobedience of Africa and white America to God's will.

4. Steward, *Twenty-two Years a Slave,* 339.

5. Henry Highland Garnet, "Eulogy of John Brown," cited in Earl Ofari, *"Let Resistance Be Your Motto": The Life and Thought of Henry Highland Garnet* (Boston: Beacon Press, 1972), 186.

6. Henry Highland Garnet, "A Memorial Discourse Delivered in the Hall of the House of Representatives, February 12, 1865," in *Black Writers of America,* ed. Richard Barksdale and Kenneth Kinnamon (New York: Macmillan, 1972), 273.

7. Rev. H. Easton, "A Treatise on the Intellectual Character and Civil and Political Condition of the Colored People of the United States; and the Prejudice Exercised Towards Them," in *Negro Protest Pamphlets: A Compendium,* ed. Dorothy Porter (1837; reprint, New York: Arno Press and New York Times, 1969), 28.

8. *Minutes and Proceedings of the First Annual Meeting of the American Moral Reform Society,* in *Early Negro Writing,* 206.

9. William Hamilton, "Opening Speech before the Fourth Annual Negro Convention, New York City, June 2–13, 1834" (1834; reprint, New York: Arno Press and New York Times, 1969), 3.

10. Steward, *Twenty-two Years a Slave,* 323.

11. Otis Ammidan and Isaac Barton, "A Circular to the People of the United States, by order of the Acting Committee of the American Convention for Promoting the Abolition of Slavery; and Improving the Condition of the African Race," *Genius of Universal Emancipation,* March 25, 1825.

12. William Wells Brown, "Lecture Delivered before the Female Anti-Slavery Society of Salem, November 14, 1847," in *The Narrative of William Wells Brown, a Fugitive Slave* (1847; reprint, Reading, Mass.: Addison-Wesley, 1969), 82.

13. William Wells Brown to Capt. Enoch Price, from London, September 14, 1849; printed in the *Liberator*, November 23, 1849.

14. Ammidan and Barton, "A Circular to the People of the United States."

15. William Wells Brown, "Lecture Delivered before the Female Anti-Slavery Society," 91.

16. Ibid.

17. William J. Watkins, "Our Rights as Men—An Address Delivered in Boston before the Legislative Committee of the Militia, February 24, 1853," in *Negro Protest Pamphlets*, 17.

18. William Whipper, "Statement to the American People," in *Minutes and Proceedings of the First Annual Meeting of the American Moral Reform Society,* August 14–19, 1837, in *Early Negro Writing,* 206.

19. *Proceedings of the Convention of Free Persons of Colour,* 1830, 9.

20. Henry Highland Garnet, "Speech Delivered at the Seventh Anniversary of the American Anti-Slavery Society" (1840), in Ofari, *"Let Resistance Be Your Motto,"* 128.

21. Frederick Douglass, "The Present and Future of the Colored Race in America," in *Negro Social and Political Thought,* 272.

22. *Conventional Address of the Second Annual Convention for the Improvement of the Free People of Color* (1832; reprint, New York: Arno Press and New York Times, 1969), 36.

23. Thomas Hamilton, editorial, *Anglo-African Magazine* 1, no. 1 (January 1859): 2.

24. *Conventional Address of the Second Annual Convention for the Improvement of the Free People of Color* (1832), 36.

25. *Conventional Address of the First Annual Convention of the People of Colour* (1830), 13, in *Proceedings of the Convention of Free Persons of Colour.*

26. Ibid.; italics added.

27. *Minutes of the Fourth Annual Convention for the Improvement of the Free People of Color in the United States* (1834), 28; reprinted in *Minutes and Proceedings of the National Negro Conventions, 1830–1864,* ed. Howard Bell (New York: Arno Press and New York Times, 1969), 28.

28. Ibid., 30.

29. Rev. J. W. C. Pennington, "The Great Conflict Requires Great Faith," *Anglo-African Magazine* 1, no. 11 (November 1859): 344.

30. *Frederick Douglass' Monthly,* January 1859, 2.

31. *Minutes of the National Convention of Colored Citizens, held at Buffalo, N.Y., August 15–19, 1843* (1843; reprint, New York: Arno Press and New York Times, 1969), 5.

5. The Virtue of Fortitude—"Keepin' On a-Keepin' On"

1. Pieper, *The Four Cardinal Virtues,* 123.

2. William Watkins, "Address Delivered before the Moral Reform Society in Philadelphia, August 8, 1836," in *Early Negro Writing,* 166.

3. James Forten Jr., "An Address Delivered before the Ladies' Anti-Slavery Society of Philadelphia, April 14, 1836," Schomburg Center for Research in Afro-American Culture.

4. Nathaniel Paul, "An Address Delivered on the Celebration of the Abolition of Slavery, in the State of New York, July 5, 1827," in *Negro Protest Pamphlets,* 22–23.

5. Stewart, *The Productions of Mrs. Maria Stewart,* 73.

6. *Conventional Address of the Second Annual Convention of Free People of Color,* 34.

7. Robert Gordon, "Intellectual Culture," *Anglo-African Magazine* 1, no. 6 (June 1859): 188.

8. Peter Berger and Thomas Luckmann, *The Social Construction of Reality* (Garden City, N.Y.: Anchor Books, 1966).

9. Gordon, "Intellectual Culture," 190.

10. M. H. Freeman, "The Educational Wants of the Free Colored People," *Anglo-African Magazine* 1, no. 4 (April 1859): 115; italics added.

11. *Minutes of the Fifth Annual Convention for the Improvement of the Free People of Colour in the United States, held in the Wesley Church, Philadelphia, June 1–5, 1835* (1835; reprint, New York: Arno Press and the New York Times, 1969), 18.

12. In this regard the author of "A Word to Our People" anticipates what Gayraud Wilmore terms the "legitimate secularity of black faith," given voice notably by Alexander Crummell, who believed that the sacred and the profane roles of the black church ought to be united in concern for economic and political issues that affected parishioners. See Gayraud Wilmore, *Black Religion and Black Radicalism: An Interpretation of the Religious History of Afro-American People,* 2d ed. (Maryknoll, N.Y.: Orbis, 1983), 115.

13. "A Word to Our People," *Anglo-African Magazine* 1, no. 9 (September 1859): 294.

14. Ibid.

15. Steward, *Twenty-two Years a Slave,* 332.

16. Pennington, "The Self-Redeeming Power of the Colored Races of the World," 115.

6. Temperance and the Quest for Character

1. Pieper, *The Four Cardinal Virtues,* 164.

2. Macquarie, *Dictionary of Christian Ethics,* 338.

3. Watkins, "Address Delivered before the Moral Reform Society in Philadelphia, August 8, 1836," 165.

4. James Forten Jr., "An Address Delivered before the American Moral Reform Society," August 17, 1837, in *Early Negro Writing,* 226.

5. Corr, "Address Delivered before the Humane Mechanics," 148.

6. Ibid.

7. Ibid., 147.

8. Leonard I. Sweet, *Black Images of America, 1784–1870* (New York: Norton, 1976), 129.

9. Editorial, *Colored American—The Weekly Advocate,* January 7, 1837.

10. Stewart, *The Productions of Mrs. Maria Stewart,* 68.

11. Ibid., 39.

12. Ibid., 15.

13. Ibid., 61.

14. Nathaniel Paul, "An Address Delivered on the Celebration of the Abolition of Slavery, in the State of New York, July 5, 1827," in *Negro Protest Pamphlets,* 18.

15. Ibid., 19.

16. Frederick Douglass, "What Are the Colored People Doing for Themselves?" in *Negro Social and Political Thought,* 207.

17. Garnet, "The Past and the Present Condition and the Destiny of the Colored Race," in *Negro Social and Political Thought,* 201.

7. Virtue behind the Veil of Secrecy

1. A. E. Bush and P. L. Dorman, eds., *History of the Mosaic Templars of America—Its Founders and Officials* (Little Rock, Ark.: Central Printing Co., 1924), 187.

2. Alvin J. Schmidt and Nicholas Babchuk, "The Unbrotherly Brotherhood: Discrimination in Fraternal Orders," *Phylon* 34, no. 3 (1973): 275–82.

3. Frank H. Hankins, "Secret Societies," in *Encyclopedia of the Social Sciences* (New York: Macmillan, 1933), 6:423.

4. Kurt H. Wolff, ed. and trans., *The Sociology of Georg Simmel* (New York: Free Press, 1950), 330.

5. Ibid., 345, 360.

6. Hankins, "Masonry," in *Encyclopedia of the Social Sciences,* 10:177–84.

7. Carl Degler, *Out of Our Past: The Forces That Shaped Modern America* (New York: Harper & Row, 1959), 41.

8. *Encyclopedia Americana International* (Danbury, Conn.: N.p., 1995), 18:432.

9. Kaplan, *The Black Presence,* 181.

10. Loretta J. Williams, *Black Freemasonry and Middle Class Realities* (Columbia: University of Missouri Press, 1980), 13; Harry E. Davis, *A History of Freemasonry Among Negroes in America* (United Supreme Council, Ancient and Accepted Scottish Rite of Freemasonry, Northern Jurisdiction, USA, 1946), 14; Harold Van Voorhis, *Negro Masonry in the United States* (New York: Henry Emerson, 1949), 24.

11. Kaplan, *The Black Presence,* 183; see also Charles H. Wesley, *Prince Hall: Life and Legacy* (Philadelphia: Afro-American Historical and Cultural Museum, 1977), 4.

12. Loretta J. Williams, *Black Freemasonry and Middle Class Realities,* 17.

13. Voorhis, *Negro Masonry in the United States,* 29.

14. Loretta J. Williams, *Black Freemasonry and Middle Class Realities,* 39.

15. Saunders Redding, *They Came in Chains* (New York: J. B. Lippincott, 1950), 139.

16. Voorhis, *Negro Masonry in the United States,* 27.

17. Davis, *A History of Freemasonry Among Negroes in America,* 431.

18. Meier and Rudwick, *From Plantation to Ghetto,* 108.

19. Prince Hall, "A Charge Delivered to the Brethren of the African Lodge on the 25th of June, 1792," in *Early Negro Writing,* 68–69.

20. W. E. B. DuBois, *The Philadelphia Negro* (1899; reprint, Millwood, N.Y.: Thomson Organization, 1973), 222.

21. Edward N. Palmer, "Negro Secret Societies," *Social Forces* 23 (1944–45): 208.

22. Charles B. Wilson, *The Official Manual and History of the Grand United Order of Odd Fellows in America* (Philadelphia: N.p., 1894), 22.

23. Ibid.

24. Rev. Benjamin W. Arnett, "Biennial Oration before the Second Biennial Movable Committee, Grand United Order of Odd Fellows," October 10, 1894 (Schomburg Collection, New York City Public Library), microfiche, p. 4.

25. Ibid., 10.

26. Ibid., 15–16.

27. Ibid., 4.

28. Ibid., 21.

29. Ibid., 13.

30. Charles B. Wilson, *The Official Manual and History of the Grand United Order of Odd Fellows in America,* 22.

31. Ibid., 39.

32. Arnett, "Biennial Oration," 14.

33. J. W. C. Pennington with Abraham Williams and William Rich, "Report on Temperance," in *Minutes and Proceedings of the Third Annual Convention for the Improvement of the People of Color in these United States, Philadelphia, June 3–13, 1833* (1833; reprint, New York: Arno Press and New York Times, 1969), 17.

34. Benjamin Quarles, *Black Abolitionists* (New York: Oxford University Press, 1969), 96–97.

35. Howard Turner, *Turner's History of the Independent Order of the Good Samaritans and Daughters of Samaria* (Washington, D.C.: N.p., 1881; Schomburg Collection, New York Public Library), microfiche, p. 26.

36. Ibid., 63.

37. William Ferguson, *Fifty Million Brothers* (New York: Farrar and Rinehart, 1937).

38. Ibid., 185.

39. Turner, *Turner's History of the Independent Order of the Good Samaritans and Daughters of Samaria,* 21.

40. James D. Watkinson, "William Washington Browne and the True Reformers of Richmond, Virginia," *Virginia Magazine of History and Biography* 97 (July 1989): 377–78.

41. W. P. Burrell and D. E. Johnson, *Twenty-five Years History of the Grand Fountain of the United Order of True Reformers, 1881–1905* (Richmond: N.p., 1909), 23.

42. Carter G. Woodson, "Insurance Business Among Negroes," *Journal of Negro History* 14, no. 2 (1929): 210.

43. Watkinson, "William Washington Browne and the True Reformers of Richmond, Virginia," 378.

44. John Hope Franklin, *From Slavery to Freedom*, 3d ed. (New York: Knopf, 1967), 226–27.

45. J. L. Brown, *Ritual of the Knights of Wise Men* (Nashville: J. L. Brown, 1881; Schomburg Center for Research in Afro-American Culture), microfilm, p. 3.

46. *Manual of the International Order of the Twelve, Knights and Daughters of Tabor* (ca. 1881; Schomburg Center for Research in Afro-American Culture), microfilm, pp. 7–13.

47. Palmer, "Negro Secret Societies," 207.

48. *Minutes of the Grand Temple and Tabernacle, International Order of Twelve, Knights and Daughters of Tabor, 18th Grand Session, September 13–16, 1920, Macon, Ga.* (1920; Schomburg Center for Research in Afro-American Culture), microfilm, p. 7.

49. Ibid., 8–9.

50. Ferguson, *Fifty Million Brothers*, 74.

51. E. A. Williams, S. W. Green, and Joseph L. Jones, *History and Manual of the Colored Knights of Pythias of North and South America, Europe, Asia, and Africa Inclusive* (Nashville: National Baptist Publishing Board, 1917), 27.

52. Ibid., 10.

53. Ibid., 3.

54. Booker T. Washington, *The Story of the Negro*, vol. 2 (New York: Peter Smith, 1940), 169–70.

55. Ibid., 157.

56. *Minutes of the 19th Grand Session of the Grand Temple and Tabernacle of the Georgia Jurisdiction of the International Order of Twelve, Knights and Daughters of Tabor*, September 12–15, 1921, Valdosta, Georgia (Schomburg Center for Research in Afro-American Culture, 1921), microfilm, p. 11.

8. Virtue and the Promise for a New People

1. W. H. Crogman, *Talks for the Times* (Cincinnati: Jennings and Pye, 1896), 117.

2. W. E. B. DuBois and Augustus G. Dill, eds., *Morals and Manners Among Negro Americans* (Atlanta: Atlanta University Press, 1914), 7.

3. Crogman, *Talks for the Times*, 45.

4. Rev. Isaac W. Brinckerhoff, *Advice to Freedmen* (1864; reprint, New York: AMS Press, 1980), 2.

5. W. E. B. DuBois, *The Negro Church* (Atlanta: Atlanta University Press, 1914).

6. Ibid., 57.

7. W. E. B. DuBois, *The Souls of Black Folk* (Millwood, N.Y.: Krause-Thomson Organization, 1973), 190.

8. Alexander Crummell, "The Need of New Ideas and New Aims for a New Era: An Address to the Graduating Class of Storer College, Harper's Ferry, West Virginia, May 30, 1885," in Crummell, *Africa and America: Addresses and Discourses* (1891; reprint, New York: Arno Press and New York Times, 1969), 34.

9. Alexander Crummell, "Civilization: The Primal Need of the Race," American Negro Academy Occasional Paper No. 3 (Washington, D.C.: the Academy, 1898), reprinted in *The American Negro Academy Occasional Papers* (New York: Arno Press and New York Times, 1969), 5.

10. Ibid., 6.

11. Crummell, *Africa and America,* 349.

12. Ibid., 366.

13. Rev. Francis J. Grimké, "The Negro and His Citizenship," American Negro Academy Occasional Paper No. 11 (Washington, D.C.: the Academy, 1905), reprinted in *The American Negro Academy Occasional Papers,* 79.

14. Rev. Edward Brawley, "What Should Be the Negro's Attitude in Politics?" in *Twentieth Century Negro Literature: or a Cyclopedia of Thought on the Vital Topics Relating to the American Negro by One Hundred of America's Greatest Negroes,* ed. D. W. Culp (1902; reprint, New York: Arno Press and New York Times, 1969), 256.

15. Archibald H. Grimké, "Our Apostolic Age," *Hub,* January 12, 1884, 1.

16. Crogman, *Talks for the Times,* 27.

17. William A. Sinclair, *The Aftermath of Slavery* (Boston: Small, Maynard and Co., 1905), 302.

18. Crogman, *Talks for the Times,* 35.

19. Carter G. Woodson, ed., *Stray Thoughts and Meditations,* vol. 3, *The Works of Francis J. Grimké* (Washington, D.C.: Associated Publishers, 1942), 42.

20. Crogman, *Talks for the Times,* 20.

21. Ibid., 25.

22. Rev. George Gilbert Walker, "Lines of Progress," *Colored American,* July 1909, 22.

23. Crogman, *Talks for the Times,* 21–22.

24. Rev. E. W. D. Isaacs, "Greetings to the Negro Young People's Congress," in *The United Negro: His Problems and His Progress,* ed. J. Garland Penn and J. W. E. Bowen (1902; reprint, New York: Negro Universities Press, 1969), 49.

25. Roscoe Conkling Bruce, "Service by the Educated Negro," *Colored American,* December 1903, 854.

26. William H. Thomas, *The American Negro: What He Was, What He Is, and What He Is to Become: A Critical and Practical Discussion* (New York: Macmillan, 1901), 156.

27. Bishop W. J. Gaines, "Welcome Address to the Young People's Christian and Educational Congress," in *The United Negro,* 35.

28. H. T. Kealing, "The Negro's Contribution to His Own Development," in *The United Negro*, 207.

29. H. T. Kealing, "The Characteristics of the Negro People," in *The Negro Problem*, ed. Booker T. Washington and W. E. B. DuBois (1903; reprint, New York: Mnemosyne Publishing Co., 1969), 182.

30. Albert A. Tennant, "True Nobility," *Colored American*, June 1902, 138.

31. Harry Stillwell Edwards, "The Negro and the South," *Colored American*, July 1906, 52.

32. Sinclair, *The Aftermath of Slavery*, 288.

33. Ibid., 288; italics added.

34. Rev. G. L. B. Blackwell, "What Improvements Are Necessary in the Home Life of the Negro," in *The United Negro*, 237.

35. George L. Tyus, "Challenges to the Negro Home," in *The United Negro*, 237.

36. *The United Negro*, 276.

37. R. M. Hall, "The Future of the Afro-American," in *The United Negro*, 205.

38. Archdeacon James S. Russell, "What Should Be Done to Secure Christian Training in the Family?" in *The United Negro*, 242.

39. Rev. J. A. Whitted, "The Duty of the Church to the Young," in *The United Negro*, 64.

40. Rosetta Douglass Sprague, "What Role Is the Educated Negro Woman to Play in the Uplifting of Her Race?" in *Twentieth Century Negro Literature*, 170.

41. Mary A. Lynch, "Social Status and Needs of the Colored Woman," in *The United Negro*, 187.

42. Addie W. Hunton, "A Pure Motherhood, the Basis of Racial Integrity," in *The United Negro*, 433.

43. Mattie A. Ford, "Why Are Women Interested in the Prohibition of the Liquor Traffic?" in *The United Negro*, 457.

44. Mrs. I. Garland Penn, "How Can Mothers Teach Their Daughters and Sons Social Purity?" in *The United Negro*, 436.

45. Mrs. B. E. Bradford, "Woman," *Colored American*, July 1909, 103–4.

46. Mrs. I Garland Penn, "How Can Mothers Teach Their Daughters and Sons Social Purity?" 437.

47. Mary Church Terrell, "What Role Is the Educated Negro Woman to Play in the Uplifting of Her Race?" in *Twentieth Century Negro Literature*, 175.

48. Edwards, "The Negro and the South," 54.

49. Thomas, *The American Negro*, 81.

50. Mary Helm, *From Darkness to Light* (1910; reprint, New York: Negro Universities Press, 1969), 106.

51. Rev. W. Bishop Johnson, "The National Baptist Educational Board— What It Stands For," in *The United Negro*, 373.

52. W. S. Scarborough, "The Relation of the Public School Teacher to the Moral and Social Elevation of the Race," in *The United Negro*, 389.

53. Mrs. Julia Mason Layton, "How the Colored Woman Can Make Home More Attractive," in *The United Negro*, 442.

54. W. H. Lanier, "The Relation of the Public School Teacher to the Moral and Social Elevation of the Race," in *The United Negro*, 402.

55. W. E. B. DuBois, *The Training of Negroes for Social Power* (Atlanta: Atlanta University Press, 1903), Leaflet No. 17, 7.

56. Rev. Henry L. Morehouse, "The Work of the American Baptist Home Mission Society for the American Negro," in *The United Negro*, 362.

57. Rev. W. H. Weaver, "The Educational Work of the Board of Missions for Freedmen of the Presbyterian Church," in *The United Negro*, 364.

58. Charlotte E. Hawkins, "The Christian Teacher, the Hope of Negro America," in *The United Negro*, 429.

59. Weaver, "The Educational Work of the Board of Missions," 365.

60. Rev. G. Edward Read, "The Necessity of High Moral Character in the Teacher," in *The United Negro*, 413.

61. Rev. D. G. Mill, "The Necessity of High Moral Character in the Teacher," in *The United Negro*, 410.

62. W. S. Scarborough, "The Relation of the Public School Teacher to the Moral and Social Elevation of the Race," in *The United Negro*, 392.

63. Ibid.

64. J. W. Gilbert, "The Necessity for High Moral Character in the Teacher," in *The United Negro*, 408.

65. Ernest L. Chew, "The Relation of the Public School Teacher to Civic Righteousness," in *The United Negro*, 397.

66. Inman E. Page, "The Relation of the Teacher to Civic Righteousness," in *The United Negro*, 398.

67. Ibid.

68. Bishop W. J. Gaines, "Farewell Address at the Negro Youth Congress," in *The United Negro*, 492.

Conclusion

1. Jesse L. Jackson, "Give the People a Vision," *New York Times Magazine*, April 18, 1976, 13.

Selected

Bibliography

Books

Allen, Richard. *The Life Experience and Gospel Labors of the Rt. Rev. Richard Allen.* Philadelphia: Martin and Boston, 1833.

Becker, Lawrence C., and Charlotte B. Becker. *Encyclopedia of Ethics.* Vol. 3. New York: Garland Publishing, 1992.

Bell, Howard H., ed. *Minutes and Proceedings of the National Negro Conventions, 1830–1864.* New York: Arno Press and New York Times, 1969.

Berger, Peter, and Thomas Luckmann. *The Social Construction of Reality.* Garden City, N.Y.: Anchor Books, 1966.

Bibb, Henry. *Narrative of the Life and Adventures of Henry Bibb, an American Slave.* 1850. Reprint, New York: Negro Universities Press, 1969.

Bormann, Ernest G., ed. *Forerunners of Black Power: The Rhetoric of Abolition.* Englewood Cliffs, N.J.: Prentice-Hall, 1971.

Boulware, Marcus H. *The Oratory of Negro Leaders: 1900–1968.* Westport, Conn.: Negro Universities Press, 1969.

Bowen, J. W. E., and J. Garland Penn, eds. *The United Negro: His Problems and His Progress.* 1902. Reprint, New York: Negro Universities Press, 1969.

Breen, T. H., and Stephen Innes. *"Myne Owne Ground": Race and Freedom on Virginia's Eastern Shore.* New York: Oxford University Press, 1980.

Brinckerhoff, Isaac W. *Advice to Freedmen.* 1864. Reprint, New York: AMS Press, 1980.

Broderick, Francis L., and August Meier. *Negro Protest Thought in the Twentieth Century.* Indianapolis: Bobbs-Merrill, 1965.

Brotz, Howard, ed. *Negro Social and Political Thought, 1850–1920.* New York: Basic Books, 1966.

Bruns, Roger. *Am I Not a Man and a Brother: The Antislavery Crusade of Revolutionary America, 1688–1788.* New York: Chelsea House Publishers, 1977.

Bush, A. E., and P. L. Dorman, eds. *History of the Mosaic Templars of America—Its Founders and Officials*. Little Rock, Ark.: Central Printing Co., 1924.

Condit, Celeste Michelle, and John Louis Lucaites. *Crafting Equality: America's Anglo-African Word*. Chicago: University of Chicago Press, 1993.

Crogman, W. H. *Talks for the Times*. Cincinnati: Jennings and Pye, 1896.

Crummell, Alexander. *Africa and America: Addresses and Discourses*. 1891. Reprint, New York: Arno Press and New York Times, 1969.

Culp, D. W., ed. *Twentieth Century Negro Literature: or a Cyclopedia of Thought on the Vital Topics Relating to the American Negro by One Hundred of America's Greatest Negroes*. 1902. Reprint, New York: Arno Press and New York Times, 1969.

Davis, Harry E. *A History of Freemasonry Among Negroes in America*. United Supreme Council, Ancient and Accepted Scottish Rite of Freemasonry, Northern Jurisdiction, USA, 1946.

Degler, Carl. *Out of Our Past: The Forces That Shaped Modern America*. New York: Harper & Row, 1959.

Delaney, Martin R. *The Condition, Elevation, Emigration, and Destiny of the Colored People of the United States*. 1852. Reprint, New York: Arno Press and New York Times, 1969.

DuBois, W. E. B. *The Negro Church*. Atlanta: Atlanta University Press, 1914.

———. *The Philadelphia Negro*. Millwood, N.Y.: Thomson Organization, 1973.

———. *The Souls of Black Folk*. Millwood, N.Y.: Thomson Organization, 1973.

DuBois, W. E. B., and Augustus G. Dill, eds. *Morals and Manners Among Negro Americans*. Atlanta: Atlanta University Press, 1914.

Ferguson, William. *Fifty Million Brothers*. New York: Farrar and Rinehart, 1937.

Foster, Frances Smith. *Witnessing Slavery: The Development of Ante-Bellum Slave Narratives*. Westport, Conn.: Greenwood Press, 1979.

Franklin, John Hope. *From Slavery to Freedom*. 3d ed. New York: Knopf, 1967.

Fredrickson, George M. *The Black Image in the White Mind: The Debate on Afro-American Character and Destiny, 1817–1914*. New York: Harper & Row, 1971.

Garnet, Henry Highland, ed. *Walker's Appeal in Four Articles*. 1848. Reprint, New York: Arno Press and New York Times, 1969.

Greene, Lorenzo J. *The Negro in Colonial New England, 1620–1776*. New York: Columbia University Press, 1942.

Hauerwas, Stanley. *Vision and Virtue*. Notre Dame, Ind.: Fides Publishers, 1974.

Helm, Mary. *From Darkness to Light*. 1910. Reprint, New York: Negro Universities Press, 1969.

Hughes, Louis. *Thirty Years a Slave: From Bondage to Freedom*. Milwaukee: South Side Press, 1897.

Jordan, Winthrop. *White over Black: American Attitudes toward the Negro, 1550–1812*. Chapel Hill: University of North Carolina Press, 1968.

Kaplan, Sidney. *The Black Presence in the Era of the American Revolution, 1770–1800.* Washington, D.C.: Smithsonian Institution, 1973.

Litwack, Leon. *Been in the Storm So Long: The Aftermath of Slavery.* New York: Knopf, 1979.

———. *North of Slavery.* Chicago: University of Chicago Press, 1961.

Loggins, Vernon. *The Negro Author: His Development in America.* New York: Columbia University Press, 1931.

MacIntyre, Alasdair. *After Virtue.* Notre Dame, Ind.: University of Notre Dame Press, 1981.

Macquarie, John. *Dictionary of Christian Ethics.* Philadelphia: Westminster, 1967.

Mather, Cotton. *Diary of Cotton Mather.* Vol. 1, 1681–1709. New York: Frederick Ungar Publishing Co., 1911.

Meier, August, and Elliott Rudwick. *From Plantation to Ghetto.* 3d ed. New York: Hill and Wang, 1976.

Meilaender, Gilbert C. *The Theory and Practice of Virtue.* Notre Dame, Ind.: University of Notre Dame Press, 1984.

Murphy, Nancey, Brad J. Kallenburg, and Mark Nation. *Virtues and Practices in the Christian Tradition: Christian Ethics after MacIntyre.* Harrisburg, Pa.: Trinity Press International, 1997.

Paris, Peter J. *The Spirituality of African Peoples: The Search for a Common Moral Discourse.* Minneapolis: Fortress Press, 1995.

Pennington, James W. C. *The Fugitive Blacksmith: of Events in the History of James W. C. Pennington, Pastor of a Presbyterian Church, New York, formerly a slave in the State of Maryland, United States.* London: N.p., 1849.

Pieper, Josef. *The Four Cardinal Virtues.* Notre Dame, Ind.: University of Notre Dame Press, 1966.

Porter, Dorothy, ed. *Early Negro Writing, 1760–1837.* Boston: Beacon Press, 1971.

Quarles, Benjamin. *Black Abolitionists.* New York: Oxford University Press, 1969.

Redding, Saunders. *They Came in Chains.* Philadelphia: J. B. Lippincott, 1950.

Richardson, Marilyn, ed. *Maria W. Stewart, America's First Black Woman Political Writer: Essays and Speeches.* Bloomington: Indiana University Press, 1987.

Shockley, Ann Allen. *Afro-American Women Writers, 1746–1933.* New York: Meridian Books, 1988.

Sinclair, William A. *The Aftermath of Slavery.* Boston: Small, Maynard and Co., 1905.

Sochen, June, ed. *The Black Man and the American Dream: Negro Aspirations in America, 1900–1930.* Chicago: Quadrangle Books, 1971.

Steward, Austin. *Twenty-two Years a Slave and Forty Years a Freeman.* 1856. Reprint, New York: Negro Universities Press, 1969.

Sweet, Leonard I. *Black Images of America: 1784–1870.* New York: Norton, 1976.

Thomas, William H. *The American Negro: What He Was, What He Is, and What He Is to Become: A Critical and Practical Discussion.* New York: Macmillan, 1901.

Voorhis, Harold Van. *Negro Masonry in the United States.* New York: Henry Emerson, 1949.

Washington, Booker T. *The Story of the Negro.* Vol. 2. New York: Peter Smith, 1940.

Washington, Booker T., and W. E. B. DuBois, eds. *The Negro Problem.* 1903. Reprint, New York: Mnemosyne Publishing Co., 1969.

Washington, George. *Writings, III.* Edited by John C. Fitzpatrick. Washington, D.C.: N.p., 1931–44.

Williams, Loretta J. *Black Freemasonry and Middle Class Realities.* Columbia: University of Missouri Press, 1980.

Wills, David, and Richard Newman, eds. *Black Apostles at Home and Abroad: The Black Christian Mission from the Revolution to Reconstruction.* Boston: G. K. Hall, 1982.

Wilmore, Gayraud S. *Black Religion and Black Radicalism: An Interpretation of the Religious History of Afro-American People.* 2d ed. Maryknoll, N.Y.: Orbis, 1983.

Wolff, Kurt H., ed. and trans. *The Sociology of Georg Simmel.* New York: Free Press, 1950.

Woodson, Carter G., ed. *Negro Orators and Their Orations.* New York: Russell and Russell, 1925.

Articles

Bogin, Ruth. "Notes and Documents, 'Liberty Further Extended': A 1776 Antislavery Manuscript by Lemuel Haynes." *William and Mary Quarterly* 40 (January 1983): 85–105.

MacLam, Helen. "Black Puritan on the Northern Frontier: The Vermont Ministry of Lemuel Haynes." In *Black Apostles at Home and Abroad: The Black Christian Mission from the Revolution to Reconstruction,* edited by David Wills and Richard Newman, 3–20. Boston: G.K. Hall, 1982.

Palmer, Edward N. "Negro Secret Societies." *Social Forces* 23 (1944–45): 207–12.

Porter, Dorothy. "The Organized Educational Activities of Negro Literary Societies." *Journal of Negro Education* 5 (October 1936): 555–76.

Schmidt, Alvin J., and Nicholas Babchuk. "The Unbrotherly Brotherhood: Discrimination in Fraternal Orders." *Phylon* 34, no. 3 (1973): 275–82.

Slotkin, Richard. "Narratives of Negro Crime in New England, 1675–1800." *American Quarterly* 25 (March 1973): 3–31.

Stuckey, Sterling. "Through the Prism of Folklore." *Massachusetts Review* 9 (1968): 417–37.

Woodson, Carter G. "Insurance Business Among Negroes." *Journal of Negro History* 14 (1929): 202–26.

Essays and Speeches

Beman, Rev. Amos Gerry. "The Education of the Colored People." *Anglo-African Magazine* 1, no. 11 (November 1859): 337–40.

Corr, Rev. Joseph M. "Address Delivered Before the Humane Mechanics, on the 4th of July, 1834." In *Early Negro Writing, 1760–1837,* edited by Dorothy Porter, 146–54. Boston: Beacon Press, 1971.

Crummell, Alexander. "Civilization: the Primal Need of the Race." In *The American Negro Academy Occasional Papers, No. 3,* 1–19. New York: Arno Press and New York Times, 1969.

Douglass, Frederick. "An Address to the Colored People of the United States." In *Negro Social and Political Thought, 1850–1920,* edited by Howard Brotz, 208–13. New York: Basic Books, 1966.

———. "The Nature of Slavery." In *Negro Social and Political Thought, 1850–1920,* edited by Howard Brotz, 215–20. New York: Basic Books, 1966.

———. "What Are the Colored People Doing for Themselves?" In *Negro Social and Political Thought, 1850–1920,* edited by Howard Brotz, 203–8. New York: Basic Books, 1966.

Easton, H. "A Treatise on the Intellectual Character and Civil and Political Condition of the Colored People of the United States; and the Prejudice Exercised Towards Them." In *Negro Protest Pamphlets: A Compendium,* edited by Dorothy Porter, 1–19. New York: Arno Press and New York Times, 1969.

Freeman, M. H. "The Educational Wants of the Free Colored People." *Anglo-African Magazine* 1, no. 4 (April 1859): 115–19.

(A) Free Negro. "Slavery." In *Negro Orators and Their Orations,* edited by Carter G. Woodson, 25–30. New York: Russell and Russell, 1925.

Garnet, Henry Highland. "The Past and the Present Condition and the Destiny of the Colored Race." In *Negro Social and Political Thought, 1850–1920,* edited by Howard Brotz, 199–202. New York: Basic Books, 1966.

Grimké, Francis J. "The Negro and His Citizenship." In *The American Negro Academy Occasional Papers, No. 11,* 72–85. New York: Arno Press and New York Times, 1969.

Hall, Prince. "Pray God Give Us Strength to Bear Up under All Our Troubles." Masonic sermon delivered June 24, 1797, Menotomy, Massachusetts. Schomburg Center for Research in Afro-American Culture.

Hamilton, William. "An Address to the New York African Society for Mutual Relief, Delivered in the Universalist Church, January 2, 1809." In *Early Negro Writing, 1760–1837,* edited by Dorothy Porter, 33–41. Boston: Beacon Press, 1971.

Jones, Absalom. "A Thanksgiving Sermon Preached January 1, 1808 on account of the Abolition of the African Slave Trade." In *Early Negro Writing, 1760–1837,* edited by Dorothy Porter, 336–42. Boston: Beacon Press, 1971.

Lawrence, George. "An Oration on the Abolition of the Slave Trade, Delivered on January 1, 1813 in the African Methodist Episcopal Church." New York: N.p., 1813.

Parrott, Russell. "An Oration on the Abolition of the Slave Trade. Delivered on the First of January, 1814, at the African Church of St. Thomas, Philadelphia.

In *Early Negro Writing, 1760–1837*, edited by Dorothy Porter, 383–90. Boston: Beacon Press, 1971.

Paul, Nathaniel. "An Address Delivered on the Celebration of the Abolition of Slavery in New York, July 5, 1827." In *Negro Protest Pamphlets*, edited by Dorothy Porter, 1–23. New York: Arno Press and New York Times, 1969.

Pennington, Rev. J. W. C. "The Self-Redeeming Power of the Colored Races of the World." *Anglo-African Magazine* 1, no. 10 (October 1859): 314–20.

Sarter, Caesar. "Essay on Slavery." In *Am I Not a Man and a Brother: The Antislavery Crusade of Revolutionary America, 1688–1788*, edited by Roger Bruns, 333–40. New York: Chelsea House, 1977.

Saunders, Prince. "An Address Delivered at Bethel Church, on the 30th of September 1818, before the Pennsylvania Augustine Society, for the Education of the People of Colour, To Which is Annexed the Constitution of the Society." In *Early Negro Writing, 1760–1837*, edited by Dorothy Porter, 87–95. Boston: Beacon Press, 1971.

Sidney, Joseph. "An Oration Commemorative of the Abolition of the Slave Trade in the United States; delivered before the Wilberforce Philanthropic Association, in the City of New York, on the Second of January, 1809." In *Early Negro Writing, 1760–1837*, edited by Dorothy Porter, 356–64. Boston: Beacon Press, 1971.

Stewart, Maria. "Address Delivered at the Masonic Hall, Feb. 27, 1833." In *The Productions of Mrs. Maria W. Stewart*, 60–65. Boston: Friends of Freedom and Virtue, 1835.

———. "Religion and the Pure Principles of Morality, the Sure Foundation on Which We Must Build." In *The Productions of Mrs. Maria W. Stewart*, 1–10. Boston: Friends of Freedom and Virtue, 1835.

Watkins, William J. "Our Rights as Men—An Address Delivered in Boston Before the Legislative Committee of the Militia, February 24, 1853." In *Negro Protest Pamphlets*, edited by Dorothy Porter, 1–21. New York: Arno Press and New York Times, 1969.

Williams, Peter. "An Oration on the Abolition of the Slave Trade, Delivered in the African Church in the City of New York, January 1, 1808." In *Early Negro Writing, 1760–1837*, edited by Dorothy Porter, 343–54. Boston: Beacon Press, 1971.

Manuals and Constitutions of Organizations

Brown, J. L. *Ritual of the Knights of Wise Men*. Nashville: J. L. Brown, 1881.

Constitution and By-Laws of the Brotherly Union Society, instituted, April 1833. In *Early Negro Writing, 1760–1837*, edited by Dorothy Porter. Boston: Beacon Press, 1971.

Constitution and Rules to Be Observed and Kept by the Friendly Society of St. Thomas' African Church, of Philadelphia, 1797. In *Early Negro Writing, 1760–1837*, edited by Dorothy Porter. Boston: Beacon Press, 1971.

Constitution of the African Benevolent Society, 1808. In *Early Negro Writing, 1760–1837,* edited by Dorothy Porter. Boston: Beacon Press, 1971.

Constitution of the African Marine Fund, for the Relief of the Distressed Orphans, and Poor Members of This Fund, 1810. In *Early Negro Writing, 1760–1837,* edited by Dorothy Porter. Boston: Beacon Press, 1971.

Constitution of the American Society of Free Persons of Colour, for improving Their Condition in the United States; for Purchasing Lands; and for the Establishment of a Settlement in Upper Canada. In *Early Negro Writing, 1760–1837,* edited by Dorothy Porter. Boston: Beacon Press, 1971.

Constitution of the New-York African Clarkson Association, 1825. In *Early Negro Writing, 1760–1837,* edited by Dorothy Porter. Boston: Beacon Press, 1971.

Laws of the African Society, instituted at Boston, 1796. In *Early Negro Writing, 1760–1837,* edited by Dorothy Porter. Boston: Beacon Press, 1971.

Manual of the International Order of the Twelve, Knights and Daughters of Tabor, ca. 1881. Schomburg Center for Research in Afro-American Culture.

Turner, Howard. *Turner's History of the Independent Order of the Good Samaritans and Daughters of Samaria.* Washington, D.C.: N.p., 1881.

Williams, E. A., S. W. Green, and Joseph L. Jones. *History and Manual of the Colored Knights of Pythias of North and South America, Europe, Asia and Africa Inclusive.* Nashville: National Baptist Publishing Board, 1917.

Wilson, Charles B. *The Official Manual and History of the Grand United Order of Odd Fellows in America.* Philadelphia: N.p., 1894.

Index

abolitionist movement, 23, 26, 44–45, 69
academy, and church, 106–10
Advice to Freedmen (Brinckerhoff), 105
Africa, 53–54
Afric-American Female Intelligence Society of Boston, 34
African Americans: in aftermath of slavery, 129–30; assault of black being, 4–6; gender roles, 120–22; and love principle, 70–71; stereotypes of, 70; virtue and African American existence, 1–18. *See also* free blacks
African Benevolent Society, 31
African Clarkson Society, 50
African Lodge No. 459, 86, 87
African Methodist Episcopal Church, 30
African Society of Boston, 33–35, 37
African Society of New York, 35
African Union Society, 31
Aftermath of Slavery, The (Sinclair), 112, 117–18
agricultural arts, 47
alcohol abuse, 93, 95. *See also* temperance movement
Allen, Richard, 26, 30, 32–33, 47, 48, 87
American Anti-Slavery Society, 59
American Convention for Promoting the Abolition of Slavery, 57–58
American Moral Reform movement, 61
American Moral Reform Society, 16, 46, 52, 56, 59, 64, 69, 73
American Negro, The (Thomas), 115
American Negro Academy, 108, 109, 110
American Revolution, 21–22, 85–86

Ammidan, Otis, 57–58
Anglo-African Magazine, 61, 67, 69
antislavery movement, 23, 26, 44–45, 69
Appeal in Four Articles (Walker), 42–43, 53
Aquinas, Thomas, 3
Aristotle, 3
Arnett, Benjamin W., 89–92
Asbury, Francis, 32
auction block, 9–10
Augustine, 3

Band Society of New Orleans, 97
Banim, John, 100
Barton, Isaac, 57–58
Beman, Amos Gerry, 16, 50
benevolent societies, 70. *See also* mutual aid societies; secret societies
Bethel African Methodist Episcopal Church, 47
Bibb, Henry, 7, 17
black church. *See* church
black Freemasons. *See* Freemasonry
black militia, 58
black preachers, 107–8
blacks. *See* African Americans
black uplift, 48–49, 77–81
Blackwell, G. L. B., 118
black women, roles of, 120–22
Boston St. John's Lodge, 86
Bradford, B. E. (Mrs.), 121–22
bravery, and perseverance, 69–72
Brawley, Edward, 111
Brewster, Nero, 87
Brinckerhoff, Isaac, 105
Brotherly Union Society, 34
Brown, John, 54–55
Brown, William Wells, 57, 58
Browne, William Washington, 95–97
Bruce, Roscoe Conkling, 114–15

Steward, Austin, 7, 8–9, 10, 49–50, 54, 57, 71–72, 104
Stewart, James W., 45
Stewart, Maria, x, 16, 44–46, 53–54, 66, 78–80, 132, 136
Storer College, 108–9
Story of the Negro, The (Washington), 88, 101
Stringer, Thomas W., 100
Stuckey, Sterling, 13
Sweet, Leonard, 77

teachers, role and character of, 126–29
temperance, 3, 16, 41, 109–10, 113–14, 137; character and value, 74–78; defined, 73–74; and morally just universe, 75–76; race elevation and racial unity, 78–81; and slavery, 81
temperance movement, 44, 93, 95–96
Tennant, Albert A., 117
Terrell, Mary Church, 122, 123
Thomas, William H., 115, 123
"True Nobility" (Tennant), 117
Turner, Edwin J., 99, 102
Turner, Howard H., 95
Tyus, George L., 119

United Order of True Reformers, 96
unity, 38–39

value, and character, 74–78
viability, 15–18, 47
virtue: and the academy, 108–10; and African American existence, 1–18; and Aristotelian thought, 3; cardinal virtues, 3, 41, 133–34; and Christian character, 115–17; and Christian tradition, 3; and the church, 106–8; in current context, 133–38; to develop self, 131–33; and discernment, 111–15; and economic independence, 122–25; in first

postbellum generation, 104–5; and freedom, 28, 38; and home life, 117–22, 124–25; and injustice, 131–33; and love, 38–39; and moral theory, 3; and mutual aid, 31–36; and Platonic thought, 3; private versus public, 135–36; and Puritanism, 19–30; schooling as nurturer of, 125–29; and secrecy, 82; and slavery, 1–4, 28; and social consciousness, 35–36; and unified vision of life, 16–18; and unity, 38–39; and viability, 15–18, 47

Walker, David, 16, 42–44, 53, 135–36
Walker, George Gilbert, 113–14
Warren, Joseph, 85
Washington, Booker T., 47–48, 88, 101, 108, 116, 122–23
Washington, George, 21–22, 85
Watkins, William, 58, 65, 75, 78
Weaver, W. H., 126–27
Wheatley, Phillis, 23–24
Whipple, Prince, 23
Whitted, J. A., 119
Williams, Loretta, 86
Williams, Peter, 26, 32, 36, 51
Wilson, Charles B., 89, 91–92
wisdom. *See* prudence
women, roles of, 120–22
Woodson, Carter G., 96
Wooster, David, 24
"Word to Our People, A," 69–71
world building, 67–69
Wright, Theodore S., 51

Young Men's Literary and Moral Reform Society of Pittsburgh and Vicinity, 51
Young Men's Mental Improvement Society for the Discussion of Moral and Philosophical Questions of All Kinds, 51
Young People's Christian and Educational Congress, 125

PRAISE FOR *In the Path of Virtue*

"Professor Roberts reminds us that black America has its own traditions of moral thinking, ethical reflection, and social criticism. Drawing on a range of primary and secondary sources, he skillfully treats the sense of *virtue* that has long informed African American consciousness and protest against injustice."

—Lewis V. Baldwin,
Professor of Religious Studies,
Vanderbilt University

"This impressive book teaches us about the pursuit of virtue in the African American struggle for freedom and justice in the eighteenth through early twentieth centuries. Particularly instructive is the suggestion that virtue offers identity, affirms self-worth, and witnesses against the claims of a racist culture that denies the humanity of black people. Equally instructive is the recognition that seemingly private virtues such as prudence and temperance are essential in the struggle to forge just communities and enable economic development."

—Rev. Dr. Joseph J. Kotva Jr.,
First Mennonite Church,
Allentown, Pennsylvania, and author of
The Christian Case for Virtue Ethics

"In contrast to much recent compromising milk toast, Roberts argues that the United States must become aware of what erodes ordered space, moral authority, balance, and personal responsibility, so that society can create a public intellectual, ethical dialogue with integrity, while wearing the garb of radical social change, coupled with a purpose and vision of the good."

—Cheryl A. Kirk-Duggan,
Director of the Center for Women and Religion,
Graduate Theological Union, Berkeley, California

SAMUEL K. ROBERTS is professor of Christian ethics at the School of Theology of Virginia Union University, Richmond.